WATERSIDE WALKS
In Surrey

D0641563

David Weller

COUNTRYSIDE BOOKS
NEWBURY, BERKSHIRE

COUNTRYSIDE BOOKS
3 Catherine Road
Newbury, Berkshire

To view our complete range of books,
please visit us at
www.countrysidebooks.co.uk

ISBN 1 85306 563 3

Designed by Graham Whiteman
Cover illustration by Colin Doggett
Maps and photographs by the author

Produced through MRM Associates Ltd., Reading
Printed by Woolnough Bookbinding Ltd., Irthlingborough

Contents

Introduction   5

Walk

1   The River Thames by Runnymede *(4¾ miles)*   7

2   The River Thames by Shepperton Lock   12
    (4¼ miles)

3   The River Thames near Hampton Court   16
    (2¼ miles)

4   The Mill Bourne, Emmett's Mill and a Lily Pond   20
    (5½ miles)

5   The Basingstoke Canal by Pirbright   24
    (5¼ or 6¼ miles)

6   The River Wey Navigation by Send Grove   29
    (2½ or 4½ miles)

7   The River Wey Navigation, Pyrford Lock and   33
    Ockham Mill *(4¾ miles)*

8   The River Mole and the Mole Valley *(6¼ miles)*   38

9   Gibbs Brook and ponds at Godstone *(3¾ miles)*   43

10 The River Eden at Oxted *(3¼ miles)*   48

11 The River Eden and the Eden Valley *(6 miles)*   52

12 The Upper Reaches of the River Mole *(5¼ miles)*   57

13 The Tilling Bourne at Shere *(3½ miles)*   62

Walk

14 The Tilling Bourne by the gunpowder mills   67
of Chilworth *(3¾ miles)*

15 The River Wey Navigation by Shalford *(3 miles)*   71

16 The River Wey and Godalming Navigation   75
by Catteshall *(2¼ miles)*

17 Tilford, the River Wey and Frensham Little Pond   78
(4 miles)

18 The Wey and Arun Canal and Wey South Path   83
(5 miles)

19 Thursley Nature Reserve and ponds *(4¼ miles)*   88

20 The Headwaters of the River Arun by Dunsfold   93
(5½ miles)

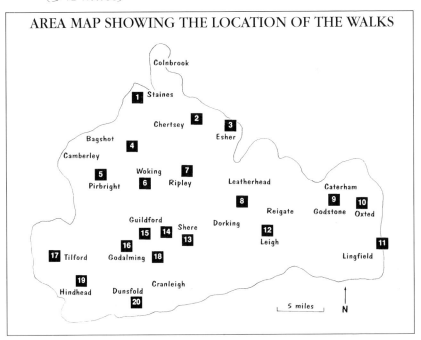

AREA MAP SHOWING THE LOCATION OF THE WALKS

INTRODUCTION

Surrey is one of our smallest counties and also, I believe, one of the most beautiful. The diversity of its soil, from the gravel beds of its northern reaches through the high chalk of the North Downs to the Wealden greensands, makes its flora and fauna so compelling. Ever since Saxon times when the great forest covering Surrey started to be cleared the county has become increasingly populated and farmed. The local Wealden iron, glass and gunpowder industries stripped the forest of its trees to such an extent that in 1574 Richard Pedley, in his official survey of ironworks in and around Surrey for Elizabeth I, reported 'great spoile and consumption of oakes and other woods'.

Surprisingly, for such a small county, Surrey has more village greens, commons and heaths than any other in England. Its principal rivers are the Wey and the Mole, both rising in neighbouring counties. The Wey has long been harnessed for its power and as an inland waterway while the upper reaches of the Mole have been rather sidelined as it suffers from seasonal variations in water level and therefore proved less suitable. In this book I have tried to capture the diversity of Surrey, whether it be a walk by the Thames, a towpath near Guildford or a stream through a bluebell wood near the border with Kent. Parts of the county that are less well known are explored and the quiet rambler may well see deer and other wildlife. Some of the walks are along flower-lined streams and brooks leading to the ruins of corn, fulling and gunpowder watermills that were largely made redundant by the advent of steam power.

The routes range in length from 2¼ to 6¼ miles and are generally quite flat. If there is a hill of note I have described the walk as energetic. None could be described as difficult. All are circular and are therefore partly by the water's edge and partly in the surrounding area. In the dryer regions of the county where there are no rivers or lakes to walk beside I have devised circuits with a 'water theme' where village ponds, disused watermills and streams are linked. And remember, each walk will change with the season. In your mind's eye you may see flower-filled water meadows in spring and summer, a brook flowing gently through beech woodland displaying its autumnal colours or those bright winter days with a hoary frost clinging to the sedges of a canal bank – but another time of year will give the route a different, and equally memorable, character.

Each walk is accompanied by a sketch map that illustrates the route but is not to scale. For your further enjoyment I would recommend you take an Ordnance Survey map with you to give added detail. Sheets 176, 186 and 187 of the Landranger series between them cover all the routes in this book and are well worth the small investment.

I have also included information about nearby attractions so that you can plan a whole day out if you wish.

The walks generally start at or near a public house. Many of these are popular watering holes on fine summer days so if you require a table for a leisurely lunch before or after your ramble it is advisable to book by telephone first (the necessary telephone numbers are included). The publicans have consented to you leaving your car in their car park with prior permission so long as on your return you use their facilities. In all cases I have suggested alternative parking close by. When travelling by public transport it is advisable to telephone the bus or train operator first as timetables may vary. Bus companies serving the area include Arriva, London United Buses and Tillingbourne Buses. Enquiries regarding their services can be made via the Surrey Travel Line on 01737 223000. Metrobus can be contacted on 01342 893080 and National Train Information can be obtained on 0345 484950.

For footwear I would recommend walking boots or stout walking shoes. These give added support and stability when you encounter uneven terrain and the occasional muddy patches. I always carry a small haversack in which a snack or drink can be stowed. It also comes in useful for waterproofs when rain threatens.

Finally, I hope you enjoy exploring these *Waterside Walks in Surrey* and harvest the same pleasure that devising them gave me.

David Weller

PUBLISHER'S NOTE

We hope that you obtain considerable enjoyment from this book; great care has been taken in its preparation. Although at the time of publication all routes followed public rights of way or permitted paths, diversion orders can be made and permissions withdrawn.

We cannot of course be held responsible for such diversion orders and any inaccuracies in the text which result from these or any changes to the routes nor any damage which might result from walkers trespassing on private property. We are anxious though that all details covering the walks are kept up to date and would therefore welcome information from readers which would be relevant to future editions.

THE RIVER THAMES BY RUNNYMEDE

This interesting and pretty walk starts at picturesque Englefield Green before descending through the wonderful oak wood that graces the slopes of Cooper's Hill. The route passes Langham's Pond, part of a Site of Special Scientific Interest where protected water plants and aquatic life abound. A popular part of the River Thames at Runnymede is followed before the route returns via a not too energetic uphill path through peaceful woodland. Three memorials are passed along the way.

On the bank of the Thames at Runnymede

Runnymede is a name that is known throughout the English speaking world as the birthplace of democracy, for it was here that Magna Carta was signed. It was on the meads at the foot of Cooper's Hill in May of 1215 that Stephen Langton, Archbishop of Canterbury, acted as intermediary between the English barons and the oppressive power of King John. He eventually persuaded the King to sign 48 demands drawn up by the barons that were to become known as Magna Carta –

7

the Great Charter of English law and liberty. For over 700 years that Charter has been the foundation of rights which millions of people now take for granted although the individual demands made within the Charter itself have long since become obsolete.

The walk starts at the 17th-century Barley Mow public house in Englefield Green. It is reputed that the last duel in England took place on the green on 19th October 1852. The two participants – Frenchmen Cournet and Barthélemy – tossed for choice of pistols and the right to fire first. Cournet won, fired first and missed! Barthélemy reminded Cournet that he was now at his mercy and offered him the chance of continuing with swords. He declined and Barthélemy then tried to shoot but the pistol failed to fire. After a second failure Cournet offered his opponent his own pistol which was accepted. Barthélemy then fired again, this time more successfully for Cournet was fatally wounded. He was carried to the Barley Mow and died a few hours later. His ghost is now said to visit the pub. The Barley Mow is open from 11 am to 11 pm on weekdays and Saturdays and from 12 noon to 10.30 pm on Sundays. Draught ales include Courage Best, Directors, Theakston and XB plus one guest ale per week. Wine is sold by the glass or bottle. An extensive selection of food is available from the bar, children's, vegetarian and à la carte menus. Food is served from 11 am to 9.30 pm on weekdays and Saturdays while on Sundays it is served from 12 noon to 9.30 pm. Booking is advisable for à la carte meals. Telephone: 01784 431857.

- **HOW TO GET THERE:** The Barley Mow is in Barley Mow Road alongside the village green in Englefield Green. When travelling north on the A30 from Virginia Water turn left at traffic lights after 1½ miles and continue along St Judes Road. The Barley Mow is to your left at the beginning of the village green. When travelling south from Egham on the A30 turn right at traffic lights after 1 mile into St Judes Road.
  Arriva Buses serve the area.
- **PARKING:** Parking is available at the roadside by the green.
- **LENGTH OF THE WALK:** 4¾ miles. Map: OS Landranger 176 West London area (GR 992714).

THE WALK

1. With your back to the Barley Mow, cross the green and keep alongside St Judes Road. Turn right into a road named Middle Hill where you pass pleasant housing and at a fork go left into Tite Road.

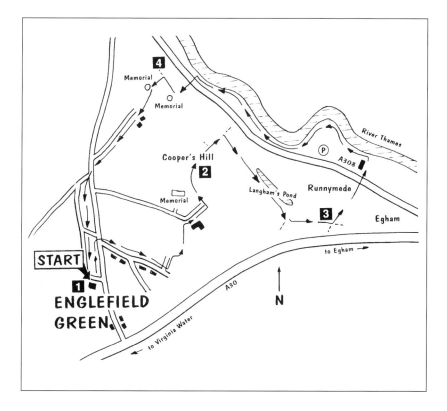

Immediately after crossing Kingswood Rise turn left onto a public footpath that skirts the rear of gardens and finally passes a cricket pitch to reach a kissing gate. From here the route is rightwards but if you should wish to visit the splendid Commonwealth Air Forces Memorial divert to your left for 70 yards to reach the entrance. This memorial was built in 1953 and commemorates the 20,000 airmen killed in World War II that have no known grave. From the kissing gate go right along the lane to pass a building of the University of London. At the end of the lane turn left through a kissing gate and continue through fine oak woodland on a well maintained pathway that takes you down the slopes of Cooper's Hill.

2. The path ends at the edge of the woodland where you should continue ahead through a kissing gate. When a second kissing gate is reached do not go through it but turn right and follow the field edge and a ribbon of trees. The path brings you to tranquil Langham's Pond

9

The Barley Mow at Englefield Green

where a myriad of water plants line its banks. This pencil shaped pond and the surrounding grassland form an important SSSI. Maintain direction along the bank and at the end of the pond go through a kissing gate to cross a small bridge and continue alongside a marshy area. In 50 yards ignore a boarded bridge on your left and soon the now rather indistinct path leads you diagonally rightwards to the field edge and a kissing gate. Do not go through this kissing gate but proceed to the left along the field edge to a small wooden bridge which you cross to finally meet a wooden fingerboard by a junction of paths.

3. Turn left on the path signposted to Windsor Road. The path now crosses a wide expanse of grassland where eventually a stile is met alongside the busy A308 Windsor Road. Cross the road and continue onwards between a factory and its car park to soon meet the bank of the River Thames. Turn left and continue along the bank of this popular picnic spot. Soon after a bend in the river there is the boarding point of the *Lucy Fisher*, a pseudo paddle steamer that between May and September offers 35 minute return trips to Windsor. At the end of this parkland section of river bank go through a kissing gate and follow the river bank until exactly opposite a memorial on the far side of the road. This elegant memorial in its peaceful setting commemorates Magna

10

Carta; it was presented by the American Bar Association in 1957. Cross the road to reach the gate of the memorial then turn right to remain parallel to the road. Soon you pass two young oak trees, the first planted by Her Majesty Queen Elizabeth II in 1987 to mark national tree week and the second, also planted in 1987, by John Marshall, Secretary to the Army of the United States of America.

4. Turn left through a kissing gate on a waymarked path to the JFK Memorial. This charming cobbled pathway leads you up the slopes between the trees to the third of the memorials passed on this walk, the John F. Kennedy Memorial. This simple block of inscribed Portland stone set amongst the trees was erected in 1965 and stands in 1 acre of land given by the United States of America. The route continues on an uphill path through woodland and meets a tarmac drive where you continue ahead to eventually reach a road. Turn left along the road and soon at Castle Hill Road maintain direction on a woodland path that runs parallel to the road. At the end of the path press on ahead and cross the green to reach the Barley Mow and the end of the walk.

NEARBY ATTRACTION
Virginia Water and Valley Garden are open all year and free to pedestrians. The great lake, more than 2 miles long, is shared between the Surrey and Berkshire borders. An ornamental cascade, stone columns and 100 foot totem pole grace this wonderful man-made landscape. Try to visit while the rhododendrons are flowering or when the maples glow in their golden autumnal colours. The car park, for which there is a charge, is off the A30 by the Wheatsheaf Hotel, 3 miles south-west of Egham. Telephone: 01753 860222.

THE RIVER THAMES BY SHEPPERTON LOCK

This walk along the banks of the River Thames starts in Shepperton, world famous for its film studios situated a little to the north of the village. The route passes busy Shepperton Lock as it follows part of the Thames Path long distance walk before linking up with a short section of the Black Ditch Walk for the return journey.

Shepperton Lock

Shepperton, situated on a loop of the River Thames, has a long history dating back to Saxon times. It is recorded that in AD 959 St Dunstan, Bishop of London at the time, presented to the Monastery of Westminster 'the possession of Scepertune', the name meaning a place where sheep are kept. An early church was destroyed by floods and a new one built in 1614 using the flint and stone from its walls. The brown brick tower was added nearly a century later. Church Square is truly a gem – 18th-century cottages, the Kings Head pub and St

Nicholas's church are all blissfully in harmony in this olde worlde setting. Originally a part of Middlesex, this beautiful village, together with Laleham a little to the north, was annexed to Surrey by the planners in 1965.

The walk starts at the 15th-century Kings Head pub in Church Square. This charming free house has welcomed many famous visitors in its time including Charles II and Nell Gwyn and in more recent times Elizabeth Taylor and Richard Burton. Draught beers on offer include Courage Best, Directors and Theakston Best with a selection of wine sold by the glass or bottle. Opening hours are from 11 am to 11 pm on weekdays and Saturdays and from 12 noon to 10.30 pm on Sundays. A wide selection of food from the bar, children's, vegetarian and à la carte menus is available from 12 noon to 2.15 pm and 7 pm to 9.30 pm on weekdays and from 12 noon to 2.15 pm on Saturdays. No food is available on Sundays. There is a patio area where you can relax on a warm summer's day. Telephone: 01932 221910.

- **HOW TO GET THERE:** Church Square is off Church Road, Shepperton. When travelling from south of the River Thames, cross Walton Bridge in Walton-on-Thames and turn left into Walton Lane (B376). At a road junction turn left and at a roundabout turn left into Church Road. Church Square is on your left. If travelling from Chertsey Bridge continue east along Chertsey Bridge Road and then Renfree Way (B375). At a roundabout turn right into Church Road where Church Square will be found on your left.

  London United Buses serve the area.

- **PARKING:** Limited parking at the Kings Head in Church Square or plenty of free parking is available in Manor Park, Church Road, near the roundabout.

- **LENGTH OF THE WALK:** 4¼ miles. Map: OS Landranger 176 West London area (GR 076667).

THE WALK

1. From the Kings Head go back to Church Road and turn left – the same applies if starting the walk from Manor Park. Soon turn left into Ferry Lane and when the riverside is reached continue rightwards along the bank, passing busy Shepperton Lock. This once swampy area formed a junction of the Rivers Wey, Bourne, Thames and numerous brooks. After the Wey Navigation was built in 1653 linking Guildford to the Thames, barge owners demanded a safer route past Shepperton

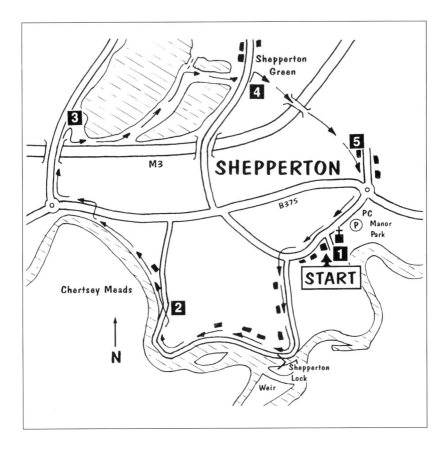

that avoided the shallows and tight bends in the area. Shepperton Lock was built in response to these demands. This pretty area has seating for those who wish to pass some time watching the water traffic negotiate the lock. Continue along the river bank with Ferry Lane on your right, soon passing a weir and the busy Thames Court riverside pub that has garden tables under a fine spreading tree. Along the way are dotted houses with enviable riverside positions.

2. When Ferry Lane finally bends to the right by a small turning area and heads away from the river, continue onwards along a path marked 'Thames Path'. This follows the river bank and goes between trees and soon passes a fine Victorian villa. Later the path passes houseboats moored along the bank. Some are most unusual – one, named 'Sunbeam', is literally a house on a floating platform. Finally when a brick wall is reached and a road is seen to your right, turn right to meet the road. Cross the road and turn left along the footpath to soon meet a roundabout where you now turn right into busy Littleton Lane.

3. As soon as this unpleasant road crosses the M3 turn right on a winding tarmac path to reach the rear of a boatyard. Continue along the path as it goes between the motorway and a lake. Just 40 yards after going through a gate turn left through trees with the motorway now behind you. Gradually the noise of the motorway recedes as you continue along this causeway between large lakes. Before reaching a bridge, turn right at a junction of paths and continue between lakes to eventually reach a parking area where you turn rightwards through a gate to meet a road.

4. Turn left along the road and in a short while just before housing is reached turn right on a path signposted as the 'Black Ditch Walk'. To your left is housing while on your right is the Black Ditch stream almost hidden by the lush growth of rosebay willowherb, willows, rushes, purple loosestrife and the occasional mallow. Maintain direction when a tarmac path is reached and soon go over a footbridge that crosses the motorway. At the far side press on ahead along the well trodden path that still follows the stream. Ignore turnings to your right and pass the rear of school buildings where the roar of the motorway is often replaced by the sound of young children at play.

5. At a small road maintain direction to pass the Three Horse Shoes pub and reach a road junction where you should turn right to meet a roundabout. Cross Renfree Way and press on along Church Road to reach the car park or, a little further on, the Kings Head.

NEARBY ATTRACTION

Spelthorne Museum, housed in the old fire station by the Town Hall in Staines, is an interesting place to visit. This small museum contains a model of Roman Pontes and a reconstruction of a Roman shop. Relics of the area's history, including a 250 year old fire engine, are on display. Open on Wednesdays and Fridays from 2 pm to 4 pm and on Saturdays from 1.30 pm to 4.30 pm. Telephone: 01784 461804.

THE RIVER THAMES
NEAR HAMPTON COURT

This Thames-side walk is about as near to the centre of London as the Surrey river bank gets. The walk is level and the paths have hard surfaces which makes it suitable for people with pushchairs or wheelchairs. Gaily painted houseboats are seen moored along Taggs Island although some are more house than boat. The walk takes us to within a couple of hundred yards of Hampton Court Palace so, if you wish, you may make an excursion here before leaving the river behind and returning along a couple of pleasant residential roads with a fine variety of early Victorian houses.

The River Thames from Hurst Park

The walk starts from a free car park at Hurst Park in East Molesey. This area was once Hurst Park Racecourse, established in 1737. The horse races held here became known as the 'Appy Ampton Races' and continued until its closure in 1887 because of the concern the Jockey

Club had over safety. However, improvements were made and racing re-started and continued until the course finally closed in 1962. The park is now an attractive open space and the river bank has become a sanctuary for swans and Canada geese. The older part of East Molesey, so named because the River Mole ends its journey here 42 miles after leaving Sussex, was built further to the south along the banks of the Mole because of the occasional threat of flooding from the Thames. The area is dominated by Henry VIII's Hampton Court Palace just over the Thames on the far bank. The historic palace and its 60 acres of beautiful gardens, complete with the famous maze, attract thousands of visitors throughout the year.

This walk differs from the others in this book as it does not start near a public house. But never fear, a fine hostelry, the Albion, built around 1858, is passed along the way. The Albion marks the halfway point to the walk and so is ideally placed. A garden and patio are available for a leisurely lunchtime drink or meal. Open from 11 am to 11 pm on weekdays and Saturdays and from 12 noon to 10.30 pm on Sundays, the Albion offers Bass, London Pride, Worthington, Carling Black Label and Grolsch on draught while wine is available by the glass or bottle. Food from the large menu is served from 11 am to 8 pm on weekdays, and from 11 am to 9 pm on Saturdays and Sundays – during winter these times may vary. As this is a popular tourist area booking is essential on Sundays. Telephone: 020 8941 9421.

- **HOW TO GET THERE:** Hurst Park is at the end of a road called Sadlers Ride. Take Hurst Road (A3050) westwards from the southern side of Hampton Court Bridge and at a small roundabout in just under 1 mile turn right into Sadlers Ride. The car park is at the end of this road.
  London United Buses serve the area.
- **PARKING:** Parking is free in the large Hurst Park car park.
- **LENGTH OF THE WALK:** 2¼ miles. Map: OS Landranger 176 West London area (GR 141693).

THE WALK

1. Walk to the river bank and turn right along a broad path under spreading chestnut trees. Over to your left is Taggs Island. At a tarmac drive continue ahead, passing Molesey Boat Club clubhouse. When a road is met by Molesey Lock keep ahead on the riverside path, passing a hut advertising boats for hire. When the road is reached by Hampton Court Bridge you may, if you wish, cross the busy main road ahead

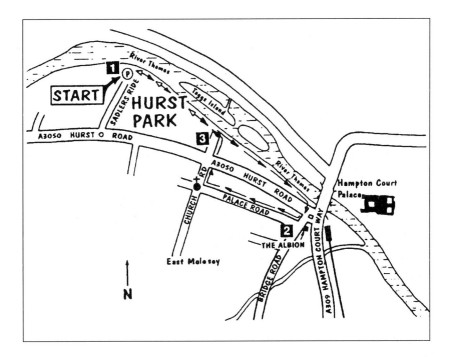

where the riverside path continues for two hundred yards or so and offers fine views across to Hampton Court. The path comes to an abrupt end where the River Mole enters the Thames.

2. Our route is along pretty Bridge Road which is found to your right just before reaching Hampton Court Bridge. Soon after passing the Prince of Wales public house and opposite the Albion, turn right into Palace Road. This pleasant and peaceful residential road is part of 'Kent Town', a private estate built in the late 1840s by Francis Kent, a Victorian property developer. Many of the fine Victorian houses still exist but some of their large gardens are shared by more modern infilling or the occasional coach house conversion. At the end of the road by St Paul's parish church – built for the newly formed parish by Francis Kent out of his own pocket – you should turn right into Church Road to soon reach the A3050 main road.

3. Cross the road and continue over what looks like a suspension bridge in Graburn Way opposite. The structure is actually a pair of gates that were used to close the road and form a crossing for the mile long

The Albion pub in Bridge Road

straight of the old racecourse. Soon the river bank is met where you now turn left to retrace your steps back to the car park and the end of the walk.

NEARBY ATTRACTION

Hampton Court Palace was originally built for Cardinal Wolsey in 1514 but Henry VIII soon acquired it when Wolsey fell from grace and he then proceeded to enlarge it. Over a century later, William III and Mary II had additions made to a design by Sir Christopher Wren. Today the building is a wonderful combination of the original Tudor and Wren's elegant design. The Tudor kitchens are the finest to be seen for their date and quite often provided food for over 1,000 guests daily. The Palace is set in 60 acres of gardens alongside the Thames. Open all year except 24th to 26th December. Telephone: 020 8781 9500.

THE MILL BOURNE, EMMETT'S MILL
AND A LILY POND

This peaceful field walk follows the Mill Bourne as it makes its way from near the centre of Chobham through fields to Emmett's Mill and beyond. During the summer the banks of this small stream are lined by Himalayan balsam interspersed by comfrey and purple loosestrife. On the return journey the route passes a beautiful lily pond set amongst pine trees on the edge of Chobham Common.

The peaceful lily pond on the edge of Chobham Common

Chobham has had the good fortune to be ignored by the railway companies and was thus saved from the inevitable boom in housing and industry that they attracted. The High Street with its many fine 18th-century buildings reflects this and has remained largely unchanged over the last century. Cannon Corner is the nearest thing Chobham has to offer in the way of a village green albeit only a few yards wide. A Russian 24-pounder cannon captured during the Crimean

War sits proudly in the middle of the grass and is somewhat at odds with the beautiful old cottage behind. The cannon was placed there in 1901, the year Queen Victoria died, to commemorate a visit she made to Chobham Common to review her troops back in 1853.

The walk passes Emmett's Mill, built in 1701 and now beautified as a private residence of some size and denuded of the machinery that once drove the two pairs of stones that during the 1850s produced 40 sacks of flour per week. Several mills have occupied this site and the present building takes its name from Richard Emmett who owned an earlier mill here during the late 16th century.

The walk starts at the north end of Chobham High Street. The High Street makes an interesting place to explore and contains many small restaurants plus the Sun Inn (telephone: 01276 857112) where fine wine, ales and food are served.

- **HOW TO GET THERE:** Chobham is 3 miles north of Woking and can be reached on the A3046. Alternatively, if travelling from the M25, exit at junction 11 and follow the A319 to Chobham.

  Tillingbourne Buses serve the area.
- **PARKING:** There is a free car park to the north of the High Street, alongside shops.
- **LENGTH OF THE WALK:** 5½ miles. Map: OS Landranger 186 Aldershot, Guildford and surrounding area or 176 West London area (GR 974619).

THE WALK

1. From the car park entrance take the enclosed pathway signposted to Emmett's Mill. As the path leaves the car park behind bear left to reach the bank of the Mill Bourne. Your way now continues to the right where the path follows the bank of the stream. Continue along the bank, crossing several stiles, to eventually reach Philpot Lane.

2. At Philpot Lane turn left and just before a hump-backed bridge is reached turn right on a narrow path signposted as path number 113. From the hump-backed bridge Emmett's Mill can be seen through trees. Cross a small planked bridge and proceed along the narrow path number 113 which again follows the Mill Bourne. The path finally ends at a bridleway where you turn left and continue along the end of a runway at Fairoaks Airport to reach a tarmac drive. Maintain direction to soon reach a public road, the A319.

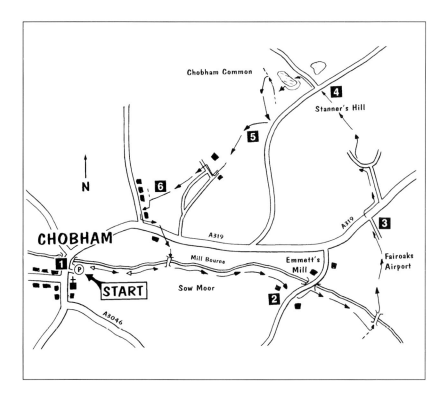

3. Turn right along the road for a short distance and when opposite the main entrance to the airport go left along a bridleway that runs parallel with a private road. Soon you pass Stanyards Farm with an unusual garden ornament adorning the lawn. Soon after passing this, at a fork in the drive, continue on the left fork. Immediately after passing houses bear rightwards on a slightly uphill bridleway that leads you through lovely mixed woodland. At a junction of tracks by a metal post bear left on a wide track that passes a house before going downhill to reach a road.

4. Proceed onwards along the beautifully wooded Gracious Pond Road and then turn left into Chobham Common Fish Pond car park. Carry on through the car park, passing an information board, and go ahead on a path covered in exposed tree roots to reach an idyllic lily-covered fish pond. At the water's edge turn left along the bank and continue to the far side where you go left over a small, easily missed planked bridge. Continue on this little path as it leads you away from the pond until it

22

meets a distinct sandy bridleway where you should turn right to soon
meet a junction of tracks. Turn left here and 50 yards before a road is
reached turn right on a footpath signposted as footpath number 53.

5. Cross a stile and enter a field where you go ahead along the left
edge. Maintain direction ahead and pass a small chestnut tree to cross a
stile into another field. Cross two further stiles ahead of you to reach a
farm track. Ignore a path on your left and press on ahead between farm
buildings to reach a five-barred gate. Go through the gate and in 100
yards turn right on a footpath signposted as path number 52. Soon after
passing the gateway to Chobham Park House turn left on a footpath
that runs parallel to the private driveway. Cross a stile at the top of the
field and press on ahead to a further stile alongside a garden.

6. Maintain direction on the right-hand field edge until a final stile is
reached at the rear of houses. Turn left here and cross two further stiles
to reach a road. Turn left at the road to reach Chertsey Road where you
should turn left again. Some 70 yards after passing the entrance to
Oaklands Farm go right over a stile and proceed ahead with a ribbon of
trees close to your left. When a line of trees are reached turn right and
follow them to a wooden bridge that crosses the Mill Bourne. At the far
bank turn right and retrace your steps along the bank. Finally the path
goes left along the rear of gardens where you soon turn right on the
enclosed footpath that leads you back to the car park and the end of
the walk.

NEARBY ATTRACTION
Lightwater Country Park is a 143 acre country park within the once
huge Bagshot Heath. The Heathland and Visitor Centre offers an
explanation of the flora and fauna of the heath while the clearly
marked nature trails take you through differing scenery ranging from
tranquil lakes where waterfowl breed to areas of Scots pine woodland.
The Country Park is open daily all year while the Visitor Centre has
more restricted opening hours. The park is situated 4 miles west of
Chobham off the A322. Telephone: 01276 479582.

WALK 5

THE BASINGSTOKE CANAL
BY PIRBRIGHT

This lovely stroll along the tree-lined towpath of the Basingstoke Canal offers variety and interest at any time of year – and shade on a hot summer's day. Along the way the route passes the 14 locks that are required to lift this section of the canal a total of 97 feet. You can choose to extend the walk through the canal ravine towards Deepcut, if you wish, before turning away from the towpath and making your way back to the village green at Pirbright.

The wonderfully restored Basingstoke Canal

The 37 miles of the Basingstoke Canal, built in 1794, have a total of 29 locks, 69 bridges, a tunnel and 2 aqueducts. Constructed in record time as a major commercial route between north Hampshire and London, its barges carried timber, grain and farm produce to the capital and returned with coal and manufactured goods. During the 1850s the barges brought the building materials required for the extensive army

24

barracks in the area. Unable to compete with the coming of the railway the canal gradually fell into disuse, with a final flurry of activity during the First World War when the army used it to move munitions. This is a walk that could not have taken place prior to 1973 as by this time the canal had deteriorated so much that in parts it was little more than a muddy ditch. After 20 years of hard work, the determination of hundreds of volunteers and the combined efforts of Hampshire and Surrey County Councils it is now thankfully back to its former glory.

Pirbright is known mainly for its long and close association with the British Army. The army owns most of the adjoining countryside and thus unwittingly has done much to save the area from developers. St Michael's church in Church Lane is unremarkable but for a huge obelisk of Dartmoor granite marking the grave of Sir Henry Morton Stanley of 'Doctor Livingstone I presume?' fame. The inscription 'Bula Matari' is the African name for this writer, explorer and, later on his return to England, Member of Parliament.

The walk starts at the pretty village green at Pirbright. The green forms the centre of the village and is resplendent with cricket pitch and duck pond which makes it a lovely picnic spot. Many fine houses surround it – some bearing the Pirbright coronet and 'P' emblem in a terracotta plaque. After passing the church the route joins the canal and continues to lock number 28 where the old lock keeper's cottage is open as a tea room during the summer on Sundays and bank holidays. Described as 'an adventure to find, a pleasure to enjoy', what better place to rest and consume a traditional home-made cream tea before the return journey? Back in Pirbright, two fine old pubs, the White Hart (telephone: 01483 472366) and the Cricketers (telephone: 01483 473198), are just yards apart and face the green so you will have no problem in finding refreshment on your return.

- **HOW TO GET THERE:** Pirbright is 5 miles south-west of Woking on the A324.
  Tillingbourne Buses and Arriva Buses serve the village.
- **PARKING:** There is free parking in a layby beside the village pond or in a parking area further around the green.
- **LENGTH OF THE WALK:** 5¼ or 6¼ miles. Map: OS Landranger 186 Aldershot, Guildford and surrounding area (GR 946558).

THE WALK
1. From the village pond walk across the green to the A324 and cross

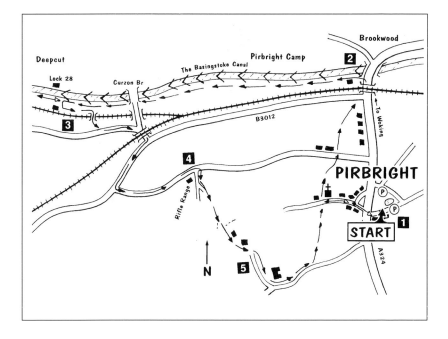

to Church Lane. Continue along Church Lane, soon passing the graveyard and obelisk marking the grave of Sir Henry Morton Stanley. At the far end of St Michael's church turn right on a pretty path that follows a ribbon of trees. Cross a road and maintain direction as the path now passes through lovely mixed woodland to reach a further road by a railway bridge. Proceed under the bridge with caution for there is no footpath and keep left to soon reach the towpath of the Basingstoke Canal. Go leftwards here to pass an information board and cottage.

2. You now keep ahead on the glorious tree-lined towpath, passing 14 locks along the way. During this section of the walk you may encounter the occasional roar of a train as it rushes along the track that caused the decline of the canal or the distant sounds of small arms fire from the army ranges away to your right. None of this spoils the pleasure of this wonderfully restored canal. When the modern and rather ugly Curzon Bridge is reached press on along the canal. Eventually by lock number 28, where on Sundays and bank holidays in the summer between 10 am and 6 pm refreshments may be gained, we leave the canal via a footpath on your left.

The White Hart, Pirbright

You may extend the walk by a total of 1 mile here by continuing along the towpath. This extension takes you some way along the 1,000 yard tree-covered ravine cut 70 feet below the surrounding countryside and which gives the village of Deepcut its name. When a road bridge is reached retrace your steps to lock number 28 and turn right on the public footpath.

3. When the footpath meets a cart track continue ahead and at a bungalow go leftwards along the track to meet a driveway. Press on along this pretty drive through trees and finally go through an iron gate to cross a bridge over the railway and soon meet a road. Unfortunately due to extensive army training grounds the next ¾ mile on roads is unavoidable. Continue leftwards along the road and then turn right under a railway bridge and immediately right again along a slightly rising road. At a road junction turn leftwards along a downward sloping road to reach a rifle range. If it is in use you will hear it before seeing it, but never fear – the marksmen are firing away from you.

4. Just 40 yards after passing a small brick building at the end of the range turn right on a broad bridleway and within 90 yards bear left and pass through a gate on a cart track. Continue along this track as it runs alongside a three strand wire fence heading away from the range. At a junction of paths by a flagpole bear left on a broad bridleway that runs parallel to a field. When a fork in the track is reached where the main bridleway goes left, maintain direction on a well trodden path ahead through trees. Pass farm buildings to meet a small drive where you now go left. Cross another drive alongside a house named The Brambles and continue ahead through trees. Turn right at a further driveway and continue along it to reach a small junction of unmade drives.

5. Bear left here and continue along the tarmac surface of Mill Lane, passing fine houses along the way. After passing the site of an old mill at Manor Farm turn left on a public footpath alongside the gates of The Manor House. Maintain direction through fields along a path that offers pretty pastoral scenes and when Church Lane is reached turn right to retrace your steps back to the village green and the end of the walk.

NEARBY ATTRACTIONS

The Royal Army Ordnance Corps Museum, Brunswick Road, Deepcut, traces the history of army ordnance from Henry V to the Gulf War. Uniforms, medals, weapons and realistic battlefield dioramas are on view. There is also a section showing how bomb disposal, an important part of the RAOC's work today, is tackled. The museum is open all year round on Monday to Friday from 8.30 am to 12.30 pm and 1.30 pm to 4.30 pm. Telephone: 01252 340515.

Boat trips are available along the canal on the *Painted Lady*, a traditional narrow boat that carries 12 passengers on short trips. The trips are available from the end of March to the end of September on Sundays, bank holidays, Wednesdays and during school holidays between 11 am and 4 pm. Longer trips are available for booked groups from Monday to Saturday all year round. The boat is located at Monument Bridge, Monument Road, Woking. For further information telephone: 01483 725527.

THE RIVER WEY NAVIGATION
BY SEND GROVE

This walk follows a part of the River Wey Navigation that must surely rank as one of the loveliest sections of canal in south-east England. It is especially pretty in spring when an abundance of wayside flowers are in bloom. The walk may be extended by 2 miles or so if you wish by pressing on along the towpath before retracing your steps and rejoining the circular route.

Triggs Lock and the lock keeper's cottage

The Wey Navigation, built in 1653 by Richard Weston of Sutton Place, was the first canalised river in England. The section covered in this walk is quite level and has few locks. One, called Worsfold Gates, operates on simple peg and hole paddles in the gates that are enough to give a rise in water level of the required few inches. The extended part of the walk passes along the boundary of Sutton Place - one of the earliest examples of an undefended manor house, built back in 1530 by

Sir Richard Weston, an ancestor of the the canal builder. He was given the estate by Henry VIII in return for his loyal support in France at the Field of the Cloth of Gold. Unfortunately only the extensive parkland is seen from the towpath. The walk crosses the water meadows to the rustic church at Send Grove which is charmingly set among fields close to the river and is a place of great beauty and solitude.

The walk starts in Potters Lane, Cartbridge, a small residential area on the northern fringe of Send. Just a few yards from the start you will find the New Inn public house, built in 1843. Part of the building once served as a mortuary but don't let that put you off the fine food and ales served here. The very pleasant beer garden overlooks the canal. Telephone: 01483 762736.

- **HOW TO GET THERE:** Potters Lane is off the A247 at Cartbridge, ⅓ mile south of Old Woking. When travelling from the A3 take the turning signposted to Ripley. Continue through Ripley and at a roundabout turn right onto the A247. Potters Lane is on the left at a sharp bend by a bridge over the River Wey Navigation.
  Arrival Buses serve the area.
- **PARKING:** Parking is at the roadside along Potters Lane. Please be considerate in the way you park in this small road.
- **LENGTH OF THE WALK:** 2½ or 4½ miles. Map: OS Landranger 186 Aldershot, Guildford and surrounding area (GR 017559).

THE WALK

Note: During winter after rain the water meadows at point 2 may become impassable and you will need to retrace your steps along the towpath to complete the walk.

1. Walk back to the A247 and turn left, passing the New Inn. Turn left immediately after passing the pub on an unmade lane and go ahead alongside the River Wey Navigation. In a short while at the end of the lane press on along the towpath and soon you pass a small lock called Worsfold Gates. Many distinctly painted narrow boats will be seen plying the waters on fine days along these parts. Where the River Wey leaves the canal to the left, cross a bridge and maintain direction to pass Triggs Lock and the lock keeper's cottage.

Soon after passing the lock a bridge over the Navigation is reached where you should turn left over a stile.

For those wishing to extend the walk – and it is well worth while –

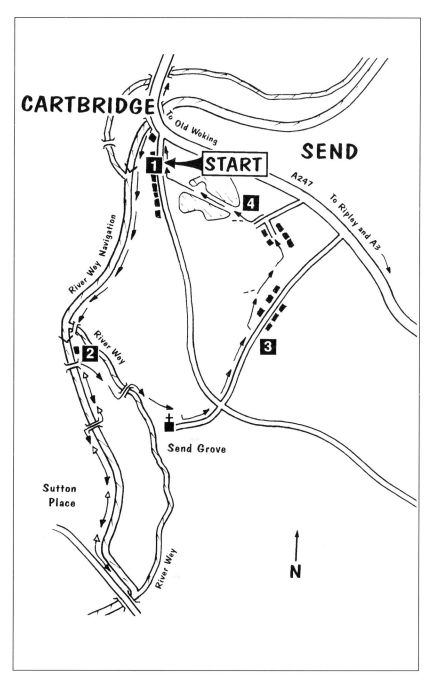

ignore this stile and press on ahead along the canal bank to cross a further bridge and continue until the drive of Sutton Place crosses the canal. Note the vertical turning roller here that aided the horse-drawn narrow boats to negotiate the sharp bend. Retrace your steps to the stile mentioned above.

2. Go diagonally right over the water meadow and first cross a small concrete bridge over boggy ground to reach a second larger bridge over the River Wey. Cross the bridge and continue along the left bank of the river and follow the path as it leads you to St Mary the Virgin church. At a lane by the church turn left and continue to a road junction where you proceed ahead along Send Hill.

3. Some 80 yards after passing a cemetery turn left on an enclosed public footpath. At a junction of paths keep ahead and when the rear of houses are reached, bear left to finally meet an unmade lane. Continue to a road junction and turn left and when the road ends by Hillside Farm turn right onto a wide footpath alongside a house.

4. At a fork in the path keep to the right and continue along a narrow, fenced path that goes between two lovely lakes where herons, grebes and many other water birds may be seen. At a small driveway press on ahead to meet Potters Lane and the end of the walk. Turn right along Potters Lane if wishing to reach the A247.

NEARBY ATTRACTION
Painshill Landscape Gardens is one of the best 18th-century gardens that survive today. The visitor is able to walk through a series of gardens – each one different from the last. The 158 acres include a 14 acre lake fed by a massive waterwheel, a vineyard, a crystal grotto and a Gothic temple. Situated in Portsmouth Road, Cobham, 2 miles north-east of junction 10 of the M25, the gardens are open from April to October on Tuesday to Sunday and bank holidays, 10.30 am to 4.30 pm. During the winter months – November to March – the opening hours are 11 am to 4 pm daily except Mondays and Fridays. Telephone: 01932 868113.

WALK 7

THE RIVER WEY NAVIGATION, PYRFORD LOCK AND OCKHAM MILL

This pretty walk starts in Ripley on the old Portsmouth Road. Ripley was once an important 19th-century staging post and later, during the 1880s and 1890s, a favourite haunt of London cyclists. After passing the vast village green where cricket has been played for over 200 years the route follows part of the towpath of what has often been called 'London's lost route to the sea', the River Wey Navigation. A cross-country stroll eastwards from Pyrford takes you to join the towpath again by the enchanting Pyrford Lock and you return to Ripley via Ockham Mill.

The River Wey Navigation near Pyrford Lock

Because of its plentiful water supply the River Wey once supported many large and extensive water mills at Godalming, Guildford and Farnham. When the Navigation was built in 1653 it was the first river in England to be 'improved' by sections of canal and created a navigable

33

waterway from Guildford to the River Thames. To the south of Guildford it linked up with the Wey and Arun Canal and joined London to the south coast. It carried coal and manufactured goods from London to the towns and villages along its route while they in return sent wool, flour and other farm produce from the fertile land along its banks. On the 15 miles of the Navigation 12 locks are needed in all to master the 68 foot drop. On our walk we pass two of these locks and Ockham Mill, a fine Victorian mill built in 1862 on a centuries old mill site. The 14 foot 6 inch diameter waterwheel is mounted internally and was driven by water supplied from the River Wey some distance away via a man-made channel. The mill ceased working in 1927 and was later sold in 1958 and converted to living accommodation. The earlier 18th-century miller's cottage, Millstream, is alongside the mill.

The walk starts from the rear of the Half Moon public house in Ripley High Street. The Half Moon has been an inn since 1752 and still offers comfortable accommodation. This pleasant free house has a good selection of draught beers and lagers on tap that include Fuller's, Timothy Taylor Landlord, Hogs Back, Stella, Heineken and Carlsberg plus draught Strongbow cider. A selection of wines is available by the glass or bottle. The opening hours are from 11 am to 3 pm and 5.30 pm to 11 pm on weekdays and Saturdays with food being served from 12 noon to 2 pm and 7 pm to 9.30 pm. On Sundays the hours are 12 noon to 3 pm and 7 pm to 10.30 pm with food being served between 12 noon and 2 pm. The pub is known for its good home cooking and speciality home-made pizzas. There is no children's menu but a small vegetarian selection is available. Telephone: 01483 224380.

- **HOW TO GET THERE:** From the A3 one mile south of junction 10 of the M25, follow the road signposted to Ripley. As you enter Ripley High Street the Half Moon public house is on your right. Pass the pub and in 100 yards turn right onto an unmade lane and right again which brings you to the rear of the Half Moon and other buildings.
  Arriva Buses and Tillingbourne Buses serve the village.
- **PARKING:** In the small parking area behind the Half Moon by the green or further along the unmade lane near a children's play area.
- **LENGTH OF THE WALK:** 4¾ miles. Map: OS Landranger 186 Aldershot, Guildford and surrounding area (GR 054569).

THE WALK

1. From either parking area continue along the rough lane heading

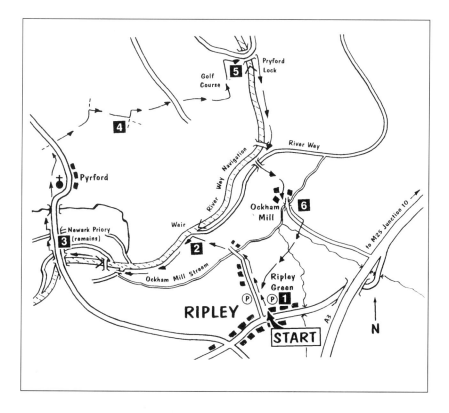

away from the High Street and pass magnificent Dunsborough House. Follow the lane leftwards at the end of a pair of houses to soon cross a brick bridge over Ockham Mill Stream. When the lane ends by two further houses continue ahead on a small path by a holly bush. This enclosed path takes you over water meadows to reach the River Wey Navigation by Walsham Lock.

2. Turn leftwards and continue along the canal where during the summer months purple loosestrife and copious amounts of Himalayan balsam crowd the banks. Pass through two gates along the way where you now have fine views to the forlorn ruins of Newark Priory, last in use some 700 years ago. Cross a small bridge and then follow the towpath over the Wey Navigation by Newark Lock to maintain direction. The path ends at a road alongside what was once Newark Mill, named after the nearby Priory. This massive mill constructed entirely of wood contained two internal waterwheels driving eight pairs of stones while a third external wheel worked ancillary equipment. H.E. Alderman in his 1929 book *The Charm of Old Surrey* wrote, 'The appearance of this white boarded erection is delightful; the irregularity and unevenness of the timbering combine to make a wholly pleasing effect'. After the mill closed in 1943 it fell into disrepair and was finally destroyed by fire in 1966. All that remains are sections of the brick footings now forming part of the extensive ornamental landscaped garden.

3. Turn right and continue alongside the road with further views across the water meadows to Newark Priory. After crossing Abbey Stream and The Bourne bridges the road turns sharply right. Keep ahead on a small uphill path between bushes to come out alongside the beautiful 12th-century church of St Nicholas. The church is almost hidden by a 300 year old spreading yew tree that now requires a little support. The church, a century older than Newark Priory, is amazingly preserved. Inside the 800 year old Norman wall paintings can still be traced, while the Norman doorway was extended in the 16th century by a pretty little porch. Press on along the road and at the top of the rise turn right through posts into Sandy Lane, a bridleway. After a leftward bend in the bridleway turn right on a footpath that runs alongside a field.

4. At the end of this path go left over a stile into a field and in 80 yards by a marker post turn right and aim for the corner of a ribbon of trees. When the corner is reached continue ahead on the left-hand field edge to a stile which you cross. Press on along a driveway to reach a road. Go diagonally right to a footpath opposite and continue along a field edge to reach a golf course. Watch out for several low waymark signs that lead you between greens and fairways. Cross a small wooden footbridge to reach a surfaced path and maintain direction. When the path ends keep ahead and cross a fairway, maintaining direction. After crossing a second fairway turn left and aim for a gate and a line of trees. About 50 yards before reaching the gate follow the arrow as it directs you rightwards where you soon meet a road by the Anchor public house and the delightful Pyrford Lock.

5. Cross the narrow road bridge and turn immediately right along the canal bank. Many pretty narrow boats adorned with potted plants are moored along the banks here and make a splendid sight on a sunny day.

Approximately 150 yards after passing a small bridge turn left by a post and soon cross a bridge over the River Wey. Continue along this narrow, fenced path until it widens and reaches a lovely cluster of houses by Ockham Mill.

6. Press on along the lane, passing the mill, and soon after passing an old postbox half hidden in a hedge turn right on a narrow path and cross a wooden bridge over a stream. Remain on this well trodden path as it leads you through mixed woodland and at a second wooden bridge by a junction of paths keep ahead. Soon the vast expanse of Ripley Green is met where you maintain direction ahead to eventually meet the rough track that leads back to the Half Moon in the High Street and the end of the walk.

NEARBY ATTRACTION

RHS Wisley Garden is a 60 acre site containing a good variety of different planting situations and offering a display of colour all year round, from herbaceous borders, rose beds, rock gardens and an Alpine meadow to demonstration plots for town, family and disabled gardens. Plants may be bought and experts are on hand to offer practical help and advice. Situated off the A3 just 1 mile south of junction 10 of the M25, Wisley is open all year. February to October: Monday to Saturday 10 am to 7 pm. November to January: 10 am to 4.30 pm. Sundays are reserved for members only. Telephone: 01483 224234.

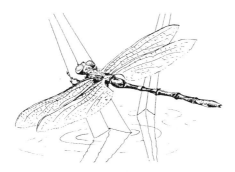

THE RIVER MOLE AND
THE MOLE VALLEY
This riverside, field and woodland walk in the Mole Valley is a delight. Starting at Mickleham, below Box Hill, we are able to follow the banks of the River Mole - elsewhere often inaccessible - for a short while before returning through the heights of magnificent Norbury Park.

The tree-lined River Mole near Mickleham

Once called the Emele or Emlyn, the River Mole received its present name sometime in the 16th century. It is thought the name refers to its old tendency of going below ground through 'swallow holes' during times of drought. The 17th-century poet Drayton wrote how 'the Mole digs herself a path, by working day and night. And underneath the earth for three miles space doth creep' and on a 1760 map drawn by Emmanuel Bowen the section of river on this walk is labelled as 'here the river runs underground'. The Mole has never been navigable nor has it had many watermills along its banks due to this fluctuation in water levels and therefore access to its banks has always been restricted. The walk passes through Norbury Park, first mentioned in Domesday and now owned by Surrey County Council with the intention of protecting its 1,300 acres from development. Many original crafts including hedge laying, charcoal burning and coppicing are now practised here. The present Norbury Park House was built in 1774 and, despite many alterations and owners over the years, retains its beauty. Dr Marie Stopes, the pioneer of family planning clinics, lived here until her death. The house and 40 acres of gardens remain in private ownership and are not open to the public.

The walk starts in Mickleham village on the eastern slope of the Mole Valley. This tiny village is dominated by St Michael's church, mainly rebuilt in Victorian times but parts date back to the Normans. In the churchyard, ancient wooden graveboards – once a common feature of Surrey churches – are to be seen. Almost opposite the church is the Running Horses public house. Built 400 years ago, it owes its name to the Epsom Derby of 1828 which produced a dead heat between *Cadland* and *The Colonel*. Note the pub sign: one side shows both horses while the other shows only *Cadland*, the winner of the re-run race a few days later. This popular Allied Domecq pub and restaurant has a superb range of food on offer, from the simple 'chunky chip butty' to the more adventurous 'delicate fillets of lemon sole grilled with a lemon pepper, placed on saffron couscous and finished with a basil and hazelnut pesto', with many fine meals in between including vegetarian dishes. Draught beers on tap are London Pride, Young's Best, King & Barnes Sussex, Friary Meaux Bitter, Old Speckled Hen and one guest beer. A good selection of wine is sold by the glass or bottle. Food is available from 12 noon until 2.30 pm and 7 pm until 9.30 pm except Sundays when it is available from 12 noon until 2.30 pm only. Booking for the restaurant is essential for Fridays, Saturdays and Sundays. Telephone: 01372 372279.

- **HOW TO GET THERE:** The Running Horses is on the B2209 Old London Road in Mickleham. Mickleham village is signposted off the A24 just 3 miles north of Dorking.
  Arriva Buses serve the village.
- **PARKING:** Parking is only available along the B2209.
- **LENGTH OF THE WALK:** 6¼ miles. Map: OS Landranger 187 Dorking, Reigate and Crawley area (GR 170535).

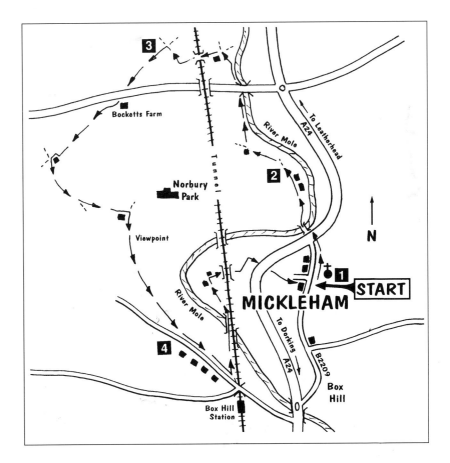

THE WALK

1. With your back to the Running Horses pub go left down the B2209 and soon pass Box Hill School. The school, built in 1870, was taken over during the war by the Army Pay Corps. It returned to its former use in 1951 and now has 300 day and boarding boys and girls. Along the way, and tucked behind a wall, we pass The Old House built in 1636. When the busy A24 road is reached cross with care to reach a small bridge over the River Mole opposite. Press on over the bridge and continue along a small lane and at a fork maintain direction ahead. Over to your left on the brow of the hill is the woodland of Norbury Park, once said to contain 10,000 walnut trees.

The Running Horses, Mickleham

2. Continue past the gates to Mickleham Priory and just after passing an unusual cottage with an amusing weather vane bear leftwards and go through a gate. Keep on along this unmade track between fields in the direction of a cottage set amongst trees. When level with the cottage turn right along a field edge and at the end of the field go through a kissing gate. Continue up a slope and at a second field press on along the bank of the river. At a second kissing gate remain on the riverside path and go under a road bridge. Proceed through another kissing gate and follow the path as it leads you towards buildings. When the path ends at yet another kissing gate and a junction of paths, turn left on a broad track signposted to Hawks Hill. Press on over a railway bridge and go forward over a grassy area to reach a field edge where you should now turn right on a rising stony path.

3. At a junction of paths turn left on a path signposted to Young Street. When this path eventually reaches a road cross to a bridleway opposite and follow it rightwards. Soon pass the entrance to Bocketts Farm and continue along the bridleway. At a junction of tracks soon after the bridleway zigzags past a single storey farm building, turn left on a broad track signposted to West Humble. Keep left at a fork by the beginning of a large clearing in the trees and press on until a tarmacadam drive is reached by a sawmill. Turn right along this drive that will lead you through woodland for almost 1 mile before reaching a small lane. Along the way is a signposted viewpoint that offers spectacular views over the Mole Valley as well as a couple of seats for a well earned rest.

4. When the lane is reached turn left along it and continue downhill until a few yards short of Chapel Lane where you should turn left on a footpath alongside the railway. Pass through a gate and maintain direction along a field edge to cross a bridge over the Mole. After passing through a kissing gate, follow the path as it bears slightly leftwards in the direction of a house. Fine views to Norbury House and grounds are seen from here and illustrate the wonderful position the house holds. When a driveway is reached by a house maintain direction along the drive. Keep to the drive as it bends rightwards past Cowslip Cottage and passes under a railway bridge. Eventually the busy A24 is reached which you cross to a track opposite. Press on along the track to reach the Running Horses public house and the end of the walk.

NEARBY ATTRACTION
Polesden Lacey is an opulent country mansion in beautiful countryside. A succession of houses have occupied this site for centuries; the present one was built in the 1820s and remodelled in 1906. The house contains fine paintings, furniture and porcelain and is open to the public from April to October on Wednesdays to Sundays, 1.30 pm to 5.30 pm; in March and November it is open on Saturdays and Sundays, 1.30 pm to 4.30 pm. The gardens are open all year. Polesden Lacey is located 2 miles south of Great Bookham, off the A246. Telephone: 01372 458203.

GIBBS BROOK AND PONDS AT GODSTONE

This scenic walk contains just one hill where the short climb could be judged as energetic but the small effort required is well compensated. Breathtaking panoramic views, beautiful woodland, picturesque ponds and fine old buildings are all here in this interesting and varied route to the south of Godstone village.

Bay Pond, a Surrey Wildlife Trust reserve

The name Godstone is derived from Goda, sister to Edward the Confessor and daughter of King Ethelred the Unready who married Eustace of Boulogne during the 11th century and was given land as part of her dowry. The area became known as Goda'ston and eventually developed into a small hamlet. As the hamlet expanded, the centre moved northwards away from the church and continued to grow around the busy green. This bustling village contains many 18th-century cottages and a few dating back to the 16th century. The early

18th-century White Swan public house north of the green was once the Godstone Poor House and the 14th-century Bell public house was a coaching inn.

For centuries watermills formed an important feature of Godstone commerce and our route passes the sites of two of these. Life was not always prosperous though and an inventory made in the plague year of 1349 for the manor in which Leigh Mill stood notes 'A watermill, rickety and ruinous, worth nothing this year because all the customers who used it are dead'. A series of corn mills have occupied the site and by the early 17th century the mill was manufacturing gunpowder for George Evelyn – father of John Evelyn the famous diarist – and employed hundreds of local men. In 1635 King Charles I awarded the gunpowder contract to the mills at Chilworth and Leigh Mill returned to corn milling. Successive millers owned the mill until it finally ceased working in 1934 and was converted to living accommodation. A lasting reminder of the gunpowder trade is lovely Bay Pond. It was formed in 1611 by damming a stream with the purpose of powering one of the Evelyn mills. Now restored and owned by the Surrey Wildlife Trust it is a haven for Canada geese, pochards, great crested grebes, grey herons and the occasional kingfisher.

The walk starts at the Bell in Eastbourne Road, Godstone. Steeped in history this lovely pub owned by Golden Oak Inns has plenty of character and a high level of service. Beers on tap include Old Speckled Hen and Tetley's with wine available by the glass or bottle. The pub is open from 12 noon to 11 pm on weekdays and Saturdays and from 12 noon to 10.30 pm on Sundays. These hours vary during the winter months. A fine selection of food from the bar, children's, vegetarian and à la carte menus is served from 12 noon to 2.30 pm and from 6 pm to 10 pm throughout the week except Sundays when the afternoon and evening serving times are from 12 noon to 2.30 pm and from 6 pm to 9.30 pm. A lovely garden and patio are available for warm summer days. Booking is advisable for à la carte meals. Telephone: 01883 743133.

- **HOW TO GET THERE:** Godstone is on the A25 approximately 6 miles east of Redhill and ¾ mile south of junction 6 of the M25. The Bell is on the B2236 Eastbourne Road – an extension of the High Street and just past the village pond and green.

  Arriva buses serve the area.
- **PARKING:** Walkers using the Bell may leave their cars in the pub car park. There is alternative parking alongside the village pond.

44

- **LENGTH OF THE WALK:** 3¾ miles. Map: OS Landranger 187 Dorking, Reigate and Crawley area (GR 351514).

THE WALK

1. From the Bell turn left and walk the few yards along the busy B2236 to reach a small lane by the pond. Turn left along this lane and press on along a path when it ends to reach Ivy Mill Lane by the village school. Turn left along the road to soon cross Gibbs Brook and at a bend continue on a raised pathway. This pathway once formed the bank to the millpond of Ivy Mill, a brick-built watermill that was the last of a long succession of mills sited here since the Domesday survey. Disaster struck in 1909 when heavy storms caused this bank to burst and drain the pond. The bank was repaired and the mill continued to work until it finally closed in 1922 and two years later was destroyed by fire. Only

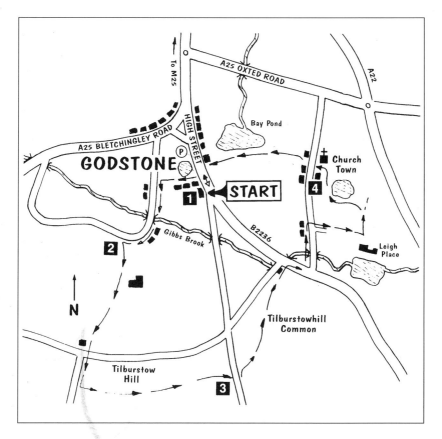

The Bell, Eastbourne Road, Godstone

the footings remain but opposite is the old mill house dating from 1698. When the path descends to road level continue along the lane until the driveway to Garston Park is reached.

2. Turn left here and continue along the drive, ignoring a left fork. At the top of the drive near the house bear right and soon at a bend go right over a stile and continue on a fenced path through a field. Cross a second stile and turn right for 70 yards and then left along a line of trees to maintain your original direction. Looking back from the top of this incline, there are beautiful views across to the North Downs. Continue over another stile and soon pass Raby's Heath House to reach a road. Press on down the small lane opposite and when a half buried pillbox is reached on your left ignore a bridleway and go left over a stile on a footpath that follows a field edge along the margin of the wooded slopes of Tilburstow Hill. Wonderful southerly views across the Weald are seen from this pleasant path. At the end of the field cross a stile and maintain direction ahead on a broad path. Eventually the path goes between low banks topped with trees before reaching a road.

3. Turn left along the road and soon pass a drive on your right and in 35 yards go right on a half hidden, narrow rising path that at first runs parallel to the road. Press on uphill safe in the knowledge that once the top is reached you will be rewarded by a long downhill path through wonderful mixed woodland. Maintain direction, ignoring a crossing track and later a path to your right, until a road and Gibbs Brook is reached. Turn right here and then left over the brook that once fed the mills of the area and continue along Church Lane. Soon after passing the wonderfully picturesque 15th-century Old Pack House, formerly an inn, and the 18th-century Old Pack House Cottage, turn right along a drive leading to Leigh Place. This private residence within 22 acres of woodland and lakes formed the site of Leigh Mill. Pass the wrought iron gates to Leigh Place and continue on an unmade track until it bends to the right. Go left over a stile and proceed ahead on the left-hand field edge. In 150 yards by a post, turn left along a narrow path through trees. Continue on this well trodden path as it leads you past a charming lily pond – a truly Arcadian scene.

4. When the churchyard of St Nicholas is reached, continue ahead on a path through an avenue of trees and pass close to the church to reach Church Lane. In the churchyard is the grave – marked by a sarsen stone – of Edmund Seyfang Taylor, nicknamed Walker Miles, a London printer who died in 1908. He acquired the name through spending all his spare time making known the paths and byways of this beautiful county. In 1929 rambling clubs commemorated his achievements by placing bronze tablets on the top of Leith Hill tower, south-west of Dorking. The plaques give the names and distances of the chief landmarks seen from there.

To your left in Church Lane is a charming group of almshouses and St Mary's chapel designed by Sir George Gilbert Scott and built for a mother in the memory of her daughter in 1872. Our way continues on a tarmac path alongside the 18th-century Church House. Press on along this level pathway and pass Bay Pond, a Surrey Wildlife Trust nature reserve, to eventually reach the road by the village pond. Turn left here to reach the Bell and the end of the walk.

NEARBY ATTRACTION
Godstone Farm is a children's farm where everyone is encouraged to stroke and feed the animals. A nature trail and large adventure playground suitable for children of all ages are also features. A lovely place to spend a summer's day. Open daily from March to October between 10 am and 6 pm, Godstone Farm is ½ mile south of Godstone on Tilburstow Hill Road. Telephone: 01883 742546.

THE RIVER EDEN AT OXTED
❦

This short walk is surprisingly rural for one so close to a busy town. The newer part of Oxted is centred on the railway station to the north of the A25 while to the south is Old Oxted where this circuit starts. From the steep old High Street lined with 17th and 18th-century houses – a partial timewarp, apart from the cars – you stroll southwards along the River Eden, passing two old mills. The halfway point is by a third mill, the lovely Coltsford Mill, from where you walk through Hurst Green and retrace your steps along the river.

Oxted Mill and mill pond

The River Eden starts life at the foot of the North Downs escarpment a little to the north of Oxted before going under the High Street where it drove Upper Mill during the early 1700s. All traces of this mill have now disappeared but a few hundred yards further on the stream joins forces with another at a mill pond where it continued to drive two mills until the early 1950s. These two self-contained flour mills stand side by side in Spring Lane and occupy an ancient mill site. The three-storey mill

48

was built around the 1850s and the two-storey mill in 1893. The buildings are still in use, but not as mills. At the turning point of this walk is yet another mill, Coltsford Mill at Hurst Green. Although viewed at a distance the construction can be seen as fairly typical of a weather-boarded Surrey mill. It is thought that this mill was built around the mid 1700s on an ancient mill site and it continued to operate until just after World War II. An unusual feature of the mill pond – now a trout fishery – is the central overflow basin 30 feet in circumference which serves the same purpose as a bypass weir but is more efficient.

The walk starts at the Old Bell in the High Street of Old Oxted. This 15th-century coaching inn is now a Country Carvery owned by Scottish & Newcastle. Open from 11 am to 11 pm on weekdays and Saturdays and 12 noon to 10.30 pm on Sundays this lovely pub offers Theakston, Courage Best, Directors and John Smith's ales on draught with wine sold by the glass or bottle. A wide selection of food is available from the various bar, children's, vegetarian and à la carte menus from 12 noon to 2.30 pm and 6 pm to 9.30 pm on weekdays and from 12 noon to 9.30 pm on Saturdays and Sundays. A good garden, patio and children's play area are available for those warm summer days. Booking in the Carvery Restaurant is essential. Telephone: 01883 712181.

- **HOW TO GET THERE:** Oxted is situated 2 miles east of Godstone and junction 6 of the M25. From Godstone take the A25 and as you enter Oxted follow the sign to Old Oxted. The Old Bell is at the top of the hill.
  Arriva Buses serve Old Oxted area.
- **PARKING:** Those using the facilities of the Old Bell may leave their cars in the pub car park. There is alternative parking along Beadle's Lane opposite the pub.
- **LENGTH OF THE WALK:** 3¼ miles. Map: OS Landranger 187 Dorking, Reigate and Crawley area (GR 385522).

THE WALK

1. From the Old Bell cross the High Street and proceed along Beadle's Lane. Turn left into a road named Springfield by the old school and at a left bend maintain direction, first on a tarmac drive for a few yards and then along a fenced public footpath. The path soon runs alongside the River Eden – no more than a stream here – where in late summer the

49

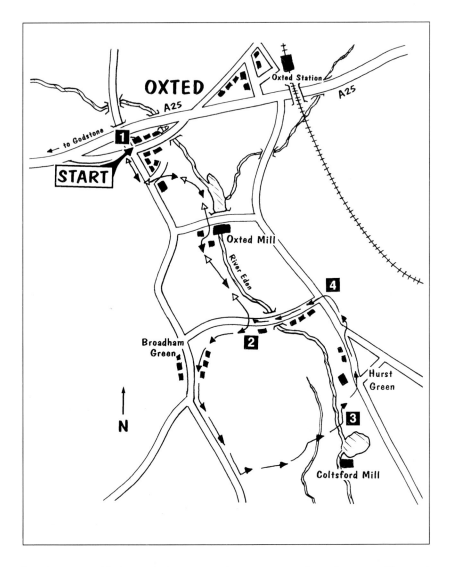

heady scent of balsam drifts across the water meadow. Soon a mill pond is reached and the two watermills come into view. When Spring Lane is reached cross to the shingle drive opposite and continue between garages and then hedges to reach a stile. Cross this stile and continue on the path through fields and cross three further stiles to reach a road by the Hay Cutter pub.

2. Cross the road diagonally right and continue alongside the road on the broad strip of grass which makes up Broadham Green Common. Keep alongside the left edge of this narrow common and bear left before a road junction. Soon you pass the lovely old Mayflower Cottage. When the grass strip eventually meets the road by a telephone box continue along the road for a short distance. At a road junction continue ahead along Gibbs Brook Lane and soon pass farm buildings. Not long after passing a house named Little Perrysfield go left over a stile and go up steps to enter a field. Follow the right-hand field edge to eventually reach a small bridge over a stream. Cross the bridge and ignore a stile on your right. Coltsford Mill buildings and mill pond are to your right. Continue along this sometimes muddy path to cross the River Eden bridge and reach a recreation ground.

3. Turn left here and continue between the river and an athletics track. At a line of trees bear right to reach a road by tennis courts. Continue left along the road and soon pass the entrance to Moor House School. Press on along the grassy strip between the school and the road to pass a line of houses that include the lovely Home Farm. At the end of this grassy strip cross the road for safety's sake and maintain direction.

4. At a road junction by a small wooden war memorial turn left into Tanhouse Road. After passing a variety of houses the Hay Cutter public house is reached where you should now go right over the stile and retrace your steps back to the Old Bell and the end of the walk.

NEARBY ATTRACTION
Titsey Place and Gardens is a historic mansion house with extensive gardens including a Victorian walled garden, lakes, fountains and a rose garden. The house contains important paintings and objets d'art. Open Wednesdays and Sundays, 1 pm to 5 pm from the end of May to the end of September. Guided tours of the house are given at 2 pm, 3 pm and 4 pm. Titsey Place is located just north of Limpsfield off Water Lane.

THE RIVER EDEN AND
THE EDEN VALLEY

Surprisingly, very few walks seem to have been published covering this pretty area in the far east of Surrey. Admittedly, to make the route circular I have had to cheat a little as the start and the first 2¼ miles are just a little way over the border in Kent. This lovely rural walk takes us through fields alongside the River Eden and the Kent Brook. Extensive panoramic views of the North Downs and neighbouring countryside are an added bonus on this peaceful farmland ramble.

Haxted Mill Museum, passed along the way

This walk, although very rural in nature, passes several historic places of interest along the way. First, and easily missed, is the overgrown moat of Devil's Den, a medieval moated manor house dating back to 1250. The undergrowth and scrub that has overtaken the site is being carefully removed to protect what little remains. Later we pass the beautifully restored white weather-boarded Haxted Mill - now a museum. Of all the watermills still standing in Surrey this must be one of the best preserved. Built in 1680 for the purpose of milling corn, the mill eventually ceased trading after the Second World War. It is open to the public at certain times of the year. Finally, near the end of the walk we pass the remains of Starborough Castle, built in 1341 by the first Lord Cobham. Sadly it was demolished in the 17th century and only the moat remains. A house dating from 1754 now occupies the site and the moat and gardens have been extensively beautified.

The walk starts from the Wheatsheaf public house in Marsh Green just over the Surrey/Kent border. This 150 year old village pub, a small free house, is a delight to the real ale enthusiast as it offers eight different draught beers – the selection is changed regularly – plus Harveys Best. Wine is also available by the glass or bottle. Opening hours are from 11 am to 3 pm and 5.30 pm to 11 pm on weekdays and Saturdays and 12 noon to 3 pm and 7 pm to 11 pm on Sundays. There is a good choice of food from a varied menu that also caters for children and vegetarians. Food is served from 12 noon to 3 pm, on weekdays and Saturdays whilst on Sundays it is available from 12 noon to 2.30 pm and between 7 pm to 9 pm. A pleasant patio and garden are available for a relaxing lunch in the summer sun. There is also a children's play area. Telephone: 01732 864091.

- **HOW TO GET THERE:** The Wheatsheaf public house stands on the B2028 Lingfield to Edenbridge road at Marsh Green. If travelling from the M25, exit at junction 6 and take the A22, pass Godstone and at Blindley Heath turn left onto the B2029 to Lingfield. From Lingfield follow the B2028, signposted to Edenbridge, until the Wheatsheaf is reached.

  Metrobus Bus Company serves the village.
- **PARKING:** Those using the facilities of the Wheatsheaf may leave their cars in the pub car park. There is also plenty of additional parking in the small road alongside the village green by the church.
- **LENGTH OF THE WALK:** 6 miles. Map: OS Landranger 187 Dorking, Reigate and Crawley area (GR 437442).

THE WALK

1. From the Wheatsheaf pub go left along the road to the village green and take the small fenced path to the left of St John's United Reformed church and soon cross a stile into a field. Carry on over the field to a stile by a gate in a hedge ahead and slightly to your right. Cross the stile

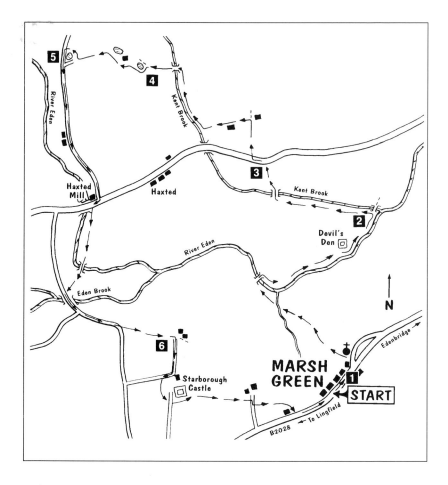

and continue on a broad fenced farm track and after crossing a small stream continue to the right on a farm track. Soon, as the track bears off to the left continue ahead alongside the deeply cut bank of the River Eden. Turn right and cross a small bridge over the river and then turn right again to now follow the other river bank. Near a Second World War pillbox and a post marking 'Eden Valley Walk', bear left to a stile in a hedge which you cross. Continue on with a hedge and ditch to your right. Cross another stile and maintain direction and follow the path as it bears right and goes through trees to yet another stile. To your left is the ancient moat of Devil's Den.

2. Press on alongside the river and by another pillbox cross a stile to

54

maintain direction. Just before a small iron bridge is reached turn left and stay along the right-hand field edge with the Kent Brook on your right. Ignore the first bridge you pass but at a second and more substantial bridge turn right and cross it and continue along a farm track until a road is reached.

3. Turn left along the road for 150 yards and then go right over a stile into a field and proceed ahead along the right-hand edge. At the end of this field turn left over a stile and continue with a golf course to your right. Soon after passing farm buildings on your left you skirt one of the greens to reach the Kent Brook once again. Turn right, keeping the brook on your left, and follow the bank, passing a couple of man-made ponds on the golf course. When a substantial wooden bridge is reached go left over it and press on ahead up an incline alongside a fence.

4. At a pond half hidden by trees and scrub, go left over a stile by a gate and continue around the pond to a further gate and stile which you cross. Press on up a slightly rising path with a hawthorn hedge on your right. Cross another stile into a small paddock with a brick barn at the far end. Go diagonally left to a gate and continue along the right-hand side of the field, soon passing another hidden pond amongst trees. Continue ahead when a farm track is reached and on a bend 60 yards or so before a road is reached turn right into a field and skirt yet another hidden pond to reach the road.

5. Turn left along the road with the River Eden winding its way through the fields over to your right. Pass lovely old Dwelly Farm and continue to a T-junction where you should turn right and in a short while picturesque Haxted Mill is reached. Turn left here by a bridge and press on over a field, keeping to the left side. Cross a bridge over the River Eden and continue ahead to a gate in the hedge opposite. Go out to the lane and turn left to soon cross a bridge and at a road junction bear left along the road. When the road bends sharply to the right, cross a stile into a field and maintain direction ahead, following the left side of a narrow band of trees. Cross a stile and small boarded bridge and press on through another field where you cross a stile to reach a farm track.

6. Turn right along the track and after passing gates by the entrance to The Coach House bear right along the tarmac road. In 30 yards go left over a stile into a field and skirt the boundary of Starborough Castle. Exit the field via a stile in the left side, cross a driveway and continue over a stile opposite. Cross this field to a stile in the top left corner. To your left are the beautifully kept ornamental gardens and 14th-century moat. Cross the stile and planked bridge into a field where you maintain direction to a hedge ahead. Go right over a stile and in 30 yards go left over a stile and small bridge. Turn immediately right to follow a field edge to yet another stile where you turn left and continue alongside the field. When the path ends at a small driveway go right along the drive for 80 yards and then left onto a small path that follows a line of oak trees with scrub on your left and a ditch and field to your right. The path soon goes through woodland and crosses a small bridge to pass a house and reach a road. Turn left along the road and in a short while the Wheatsheaf public house and the end of the walk are in sight. A few yards more and the village green is reached.

NEARBY ATTRACTIONS

Haxted Mill is a working watermill museum standing on the River Eden. It is open to the public between 1 pm and 5 pm from April to September on Wednesdays, Saturdays, Sundays and bank holidays. It is situated 2 miles west of Edenbridge off the B2026. Telephone: 01732 862914.

Lingfield is a lovely place to stop and explore. Away from the more modern shopping area there are pretty cottages overlooking the tiny pond that forms its centre. Alongside the pond stands St Peter's Cross built in 1473 to mark the boundary between the Puttenden and Billeshurst manors. The small attached building is the village prison, built in 1773 and used for more than a century.

THE UPPER REACHES OF
THE RIVER MOLE
✦❀❀✦

*This water-themed walk passes through open countryside that offers
the rambler impressive panoramic views of the surrounding area.
This is a good opportunity to get close to the River Mole - often
inaccessible in its upper reaches - and four of its small tributaries
are also crossed on this captivating ramble to the north of Leigh. The
route passes the sites of two watermills, one still partially working.*

The 18th-century miller's house, Wonham Mill

Leigh (pronounced Lye) is situated in the heart of the Weald. It was
originally one of Surrey's 'iron' villages, the power being supplied by a
tributary of the Mole that runs through the village. The traditional
green, resplendent with its water pump, has the church on its northern
boundary, the Plough public house bordering the western edge while
on the eastern boundary is the long, low Priests' House, a 15th-century
half-timbered building. Leigh is the epitome of a Surrey village.

The route passes the rather bleak buildings of Wonham Mill although a short detour here brings you to the lovely mill pond and picturesque 18th-century mill house. This is an ancient mill site and records show that milling has taken place here for at least 800 years. The last serious milling ceased in 1930 and the machinery was later sold for scrap. By the Second World War the Ministry of Food had requisitioned the buildings for grain storage. Since the war the buildings have been used to store animal feed and have remained in continuous use. Occasional oat grinding is carried out but not with water power. The second mill passed on this walk is Flanchford Mill, built on a 700 year old mill site. Like Wonham Mill it ceased working in the 1930s. Unfortunately, although it retains its machinery the building itself is derelict. Two brick cottages added at about the time it closed are all that can been seen from the path.

The walk starts from the Plough public house opposite the village green. The north wing of this picturesque pub dates back to the 14th and 15th centuries. Owned by the King & Barnes brewery, this friendly inn has Sussex, Broadwood, Festive and Old Ale plus a different guest beer each month on tap whilst wine is sold by the glass or bottle. A wide selection of wholesome food from the snack, vegetarian and à la carte menus is available. Smaller portions are available for children. The pretty garden overlooking the green makes it a very pleasant spot for refreshments on a warm day. This is a popular pub and booking is advisable for à la carte meals. Telephone: 01306 611348.

- **HOW TO GET THERE:** The Plough is in the centre of Leigh village alongside the green. Turn off the A25 at a roundabout just north of Betchworth, between Reigate and Dorking, into Station Road then follow direction signs for 3 miles to Leigh.
  Tillingbourne Buses serve the village.
- **PARKING:** Walkers using the Plough may leave their cars in the pub car park. Parking is also available along the road.
- **LENGTH OF THE WALK:** 5¼ miles. Map: OS Landranger 187 Dorking, Reigate and Crawley area (GR 225469).

THE WALK

1. With your back to the Plough public house, turn left and walk along the road, passing St Bartholomew's church, and soon at a bend turn right through a kissing gate. Proceed diagonally leftwards across a field to the far corner. On your left you will notice Leigh Place, a moated

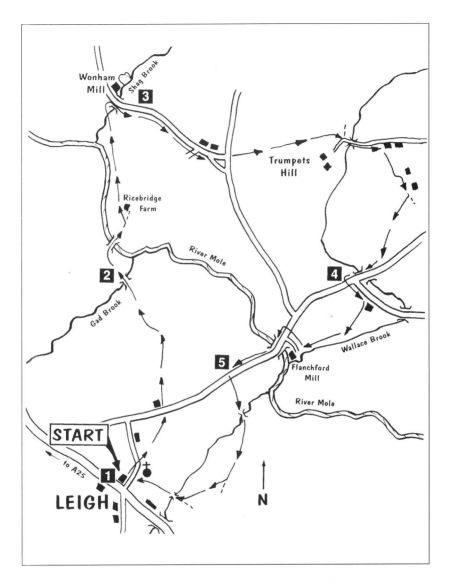

15th-century house, but largely rebuilt in 1810 in the then popular Gothic style. When the corner of the field is reached maintain direction for 150 yards and then turn left and cross a small planked bridge and stile. Keep ahead to a further stile in front of a house. Cross this and the road to continue ahead on a farm track and soon pass through a gate. When the farm track bends leftwards, continue ahead through a gate and maintain direction through fields with magnificent views to Colley Hill. After crossing a series of three stiles you reach a field that contains an old wooden barn. Turn diagonally left here and head for a stile hidden in a hedge to the left of the third oak tree from the barn.

Cross the stile and follow a distinct path that leads you to an oak tree by an electricity post and continue to a stile and cross a small bridge over the Gad Brook.

2. Go over a second stile and maintain direction across a field to the corner by a fingerpost. Turn right here on a downhill path through trees and go over a bridge that crosses the River Mole. Press on along the broad path, passing a pillbox and ignoring a stile on your right. Soon, cross a stile on your left alongside a gate and continue along the field edge by a garden. Maintain direction through these fields to eventually reach the buildings of Wonham Mill. A small detour left along the road to a footpath alongside the mill brings you to the mill pond and the delightful miller's house. Interestingly the three mill ponds that were required to power the mill are not fed by the River Mole, but by the Shag Brook, a small tributary.

3. Our way continues rightwards along Trumpets Hill Road where you soon cross the millrace which returns the water to the River Mole. When the road ends at a T-junction at the top of a rise, continue onwards on a footpath that goes uphill between trees. Cross a stile to continue on a fenced path. After crossing the second of two stiles by a junction of tracks, proceed diagonally right and continue along a lane which soon crosses Wallace Brook. Just before a house is reached on the right side of the lane turn right on a footpath and go forward along the left-hand field edge and press on up an incline alongside a house. Soon, when a farm track is reached by a fingerpost, turn right on a path that leads you to a line of trees. Maintain direction through the trees and cross a second field to a stile in the hedge on the far side. Cross the stile and turn right along the road to soon cross the Wallace Brook for the second time.

4. At a road junction turn left along the road and in a short while turn right on a footpath by a house and continue ahead along the field edge. When farm buildings are reached press on ahead to soon reach a second field which you cross diagonally leftwards to reach a pillbox and small lane. The cottages ahead of you are by the ruins of Flanchford

Mill. Turn right here to meet a road where you now turn left along the road and cross the River Mole.

5. After passing the entrance to Bury's Court School turn left on a fenced footpath. Cross a stile and bear right to reach a bridge over a seemingly un-named small tributary of the River Mole. After crossing the stream go diagonally right to a stile – ignore a stile and small bridge immediately on your right. Cross two further stiles to reach a large field where you maintain direction on the right-hand field edge. In 150 yards as the field edge drops away to the right keep ahead and aim for a stile by hawthorn bushes. Cross this stile and press on along the right side of the field until a gate and stile are reached. Cross the stile and go diagonally half right alongside a wire fence to reach another stile in a hawthorn hedge ahead. Go over the stile and turn immediately right to soon cross a bridge over the un-named stream again. Proceed ahead and cross a further stile to continue along a fenced path that leads you to St Bartholomew's graveyard. Carry on through the graveyard and go through a large wooden gate in the left corner and exit onto the village green where you will find the Plough pub and the end of the walk.

NEARBY ATTRACTION

Gatwick Zoo and Aviaries is a children's zoo where just as much fun is had by adults. On view are small monkeys, emus, wallabies, otters and meerkats plus tropical butterflies and birds. A large expanse of gardens, a lake and lawns make an it ideal picnic spot for all the family. Open all year from 10.30 am to 6 pm or dusk during winter, the zoo is at Russ Hill near Charlwood, 4½ miles south of Leigh. Telephone: 01293 862312.

THE TILLING BOURNE AT SHERE
✦❈✦

One of the jewels in Surrey's crown must surely be the beautiful old village of Shere that nestles below the escarpment of the North Downs. The village, with its close array of narrow streets, half-timbered houses, 12th-century St James's church and the Tilling Bourne flowing through the centre, is a delightful place to explore. The walk takes you past two fords and through the splendid wooded parkland of Albury Park. There is one energetic uphill climb but you are well rewarded by the views over the Tilling Bourne valley.

The Tilling Bourne entering Shere

In its short length – for it is less than ten miles long – the Tilling Bourne once had an enormous impact on this small part of Surrey. After rising on the northern slopes of Leith Hill it fed a hammer pond that powered large tilt hammers as they beat out iron artefacts at Abinger Hammer – an important centre of Surrey ironworking in the 18th century, a couple of miles to the east of Shere. Just 1 mile to the east it powered mills at Gomshall before passing through the centre of Shere village to become the driving force of the gunpowder mills at Chilworth. Before ending its short journey at the River Wey it drove the waterwheel of the 18th-century mill at Shalford. The old hammer pond is a tranquil place now and grows watercress commercially whilst the gunpowder mills of Chilworth ceased their deadly trade in 1920 after they were destroyed by fire. Shalford Mill is owned by the National Trust and is open to the public daily. With its noisy past behind it, the clear, shallow Tilling Bourne is now, by any measure, a joy to the rambler.

The walk starts at the Prince of Wales public house in Shere Lane in the centre of the village. This free house, built around the turn of the century, offers a warm welcome and is open from 11 am to 11 pm on weekdays and Saturdays and from 12 noon to 10.30 pm on Sundays. Beers on tap include Guinness, Beamish Red, Breakspear and Flowers plus Stella and Foster's lagers while wines are served by the glass or bottle. Highly recommended are a bevy of fruit wines made in the heart of Hampshire. There is a good selection of food from the menu and you will be stunned by the gargantuan size of the platter whether it be a ploughman's lunch, broccoli and cream cheese bake or a traditional Sunday roast. Look out for the 'chefs specials' on the blackboards that supplement the menu. Vegetarians are catered for, as are children. Food is served from 12 noon to 2.30 pm and 6 pm to 9 pm except on Sundays when it is served between 12 noon and 2.30 pm only. This is a popular pub and it is necessary to book if wishing to eat here on Sundays. A pleasant garden with tables and chairs can be used on those warm sunny days during spring and summer. Telephone: 01483 202313.

- **HOW TO GET THERE:** From Dorking, proceed along the A25 in the direction of Guildford and pass through Abinger Hammer and Gomshall. Soon turn left into Gomshall Lane, signposted to Shere, and turn left again into Middle Street to find the centre of the village. Shere Lane and the Prince of Wales pub are ahead of you.

   From Guildford, take the A25 in the direction of Leatherhead and at West Clandon follow the A25 signs as the road goes right at a set of traffic lights. After passing the local beauty spots of Newlands Corner and the Silent Pool, take the second turning on your right, signposted to Shere. After passing under a rustic footbridge, turn right into Middle Street.

   Tillingbourne Buses serve the village.

- **PARKING:** Walkers using the Prince of Wales pub may leave their cars in the pub car park. Parking is available around the village and at the recreation ground in Upper Street.

- **LENGTH OF THE WALK:** 3½ miles. Map: OS Landranger 187 Dorking, Reigate and Crawley area (GR 073477).

THE WALK

1. From the Prince of Wales turn right and go up Shere Lane to soon pass Shere Museum (open Easter to September, 1 pm to 6 pm on weekdays excluding Wednesdays; Sundays and bank holidays 11 am to 7 pm). Turn left into Spinning Walk and then left again down Church Hill to reach 12th-century St James's church. Turn right here and then left through the gate in the churchyard wall. Continue through the well tended churchyard and cross a small planked bridge over the Tilling Bourne to reach Gomshall Lane by the village school.

2. Turn left along the road and then left again into Middle Street. An unusual drinking fountain, built in 1886, is to be found here tucked into

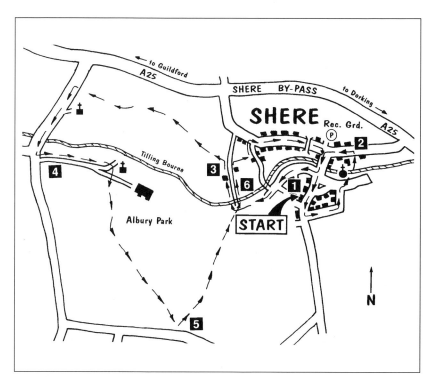

The pub at the start of the walk

a wall like a small grotto. The well beneath is 280 feet deep. Middle Street is a delight to the eye with its splendid mixture of buildings. Just before the bridge over the river is the old fire station, now sympathetically converted to public conveniences. Immediately after crossing the bridge turn right into Lower Street and continue alongside the river. Soon you pass The Old Prison built in Tudor times. Where the road fords the river, keep ahead on a wide unmade driveway. After passing the entrance to The Old Rectory go through a kissing gate on your right and maintain direction alongside the river. Go through a second kissing gate and turn right over a footbridge and proceed ahead up a small lane.

3. After passing two houses turn left at a footpath sign on a rising path through trees and at a field keep ahead and proceed to the far corner. Our way continues on a path through trees to a further field which you cross, still maintaining direction. Exit the field and continue down a cart track to reach a road. Turn left here on the enclosed path alongside the road and shortly after crossing the Tilling Bourne turn left into New Road. Within yards you should turn left again and proceed along the driveway of Albury Park.

4. The driveway leads you through magnificent parkland with wonderful pastoral views over the Tilling Bourne. Please remember this is private parkland and you should not wander off the drive. At a fork in the drive bear left and at a junction of tracks in front of the wonderful old Saxon church, turn right to meet the main drive by a public footpath sign. Press on up a grassy slope and go left through a gate and continue uphill through well managed woodland. At the end of this lovely woodland bear right on a cart track and soon go through a metal gate alongside a bungalow.

5. Turn immediately left and pass through a kissing gate to continue the walk along a fenced path between an avenue of old gnarled chestnut trees. Your earlier exertions are rewarded here by the beautiful views offered over the Tilling Bourne valley to the North Downs beyond. You can also be safe in the knowledge that the remainder of the walk is now all downhill. At the end of this path by a house go through a gate to meet the Tilling Bourne once again.

6. Cross the river and continue up the same lane walked earlier, but this time, at the footpath sign, turn right and continue alongside a wall to meet a road where you should turn left. At a road junction turn right along Upper Street. One small oddity here is a cottage named Bignolds where, on closer inspection, you will see that the V-shaped roof gutters and square drainpipes are made entirely from wood. After passing under a rustic footbridge turn right into Middle Street to reach the Prince of Wales pub and the end of the walk.

NEARBY ATTRACTION
The *Silent Pool* has become a part of local folklore due to the writings of Martin Tupper, a popular poet during Victorian times. He was the author of *Stephen Langton, a Romance of the Silent Pool,* a tale of unrequited love which included historical characters such as King John and Stephen Langton, Archbishop of Canterbury, both involved in Magna Carta. Local beauty spots become identified with the story – Sherbourne Pond became the Silent Pool, a cave at Reigate became the Barons' Cave and the pub at Friday Street is now named after the Archbishop. Although Martin Tupper claimed it to be a true story the facts clearly do not bear this out. However, this pond, fed by a chalk spring, is still visited by hundreds of people who enjoy its peace and tranquillity. Located 1 mile west of Shere on the A25 the Silent Pool is accessible all year. Free car parking.

THE TILLING BOURNE BY THE GUNPOWDER MILLS OF CHILWORTH

This energetic, varied and interesting walk discovers the Tilling Bourne's industrial past as well as its present day tranquillity. Where men once toiled under extreme danger in gunpowder mills along its banks the rambler can sit and enjoy the quiet setting as the Tilling Bourne, with its work now done, winds its way peacefully to join the River Wey at Shalford. The circular route climbs from the valley to enjoy magnificent views from St Martha's church, high on the greensand ridge, before returning via a delightful mill pond.

The Percy Arms, Chilworth

Gunpowder was first manufactured on the Tilling Bourne at Chilworth in 1580 and in 1625 the East India Company built gunpowder and cordite mills on the already existing site. In 1885 the Chilworth Gunpowder Company was formed and at its peak employed 400 workers. Although it is hard to imagine now as you pass the ruined mills alongside the water channels that once drove them, in its day this was the most important site of gunpower production in Britain. In 1822 William Cobbett on one of his *Rural Rides* condemned the Tilling Bourne valley as having one 'of the most damnable inventions that ever sprang from the minds of man under the influence of the devil, namely the making of gunpowder'. The grindstones only stopped turning in 1920 after a major fire. The woodland that once supplied the charcoal for the production of gunpowder is now alive with birdsong and offers the rambler peace and quiet away from the hurly burly of modern day life.

The walk starts at the Percy Arms public house – named after the Percy family that owned much of Chilworth and surrounding area in the 19th century. The pub is thought to have begun as a beerhouse in the middle of the 19th century and served the workers from the nearby gunpowder mills. After a tragic accident at the mill in 1901 when six men were killed the Percy Arms was used as a temporary mortuary which could explain the subsequent stories of ghosts that troubled staff and customers at that time. The pub has been greatly enlarged and improved in recent years and the extensive garden has lovely views across fields to St Martha's church on the hill above the Tilling Bourne. A good selection of food from the large bar, children's, vegetarian and à la carte menus is available. Telephone: 01483 561765.

- **HOW TO GET THERE:** The Percy Arms stands on the A248 opposite Chilworth Station and can be reached from the Guildford direction via the A281 Guildford to Shalford road. Turn left at Shalford onto the A248 and follow the signs to Chilworth.

  When travelling from the Dorking direction follow the A25 and turn left onto the A248 by the Silent Pool. Continue through Albury and you will see the Percy Arms to your right.

  Tillingbourne Buses and Thames Trains serve the village.
- **PARKING:** Walkers using the Percy Arms may leave their cars in the pub car park. Parking is also available along the road.
- **LENGTH OF THE WALK:** 3¾ miles. Map: OS Landranger 186 Aldershot, Guildford and surrounding area (GR 030473).

THE WALK

1. From the Percy Arms car park turn left along the road, passing the Chilworth Station sign, and later turn left along a farm track at Lockner Farm. When this track enters woodland cross the Tilling Bourne and

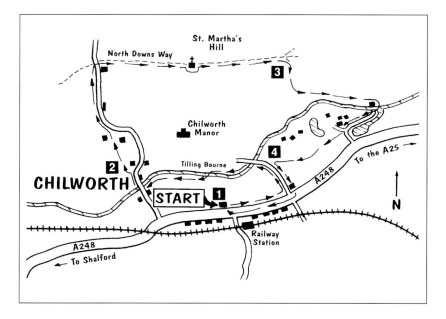

turn left along a path by an information board. You are now alongside some of the ruined gunpowder mills. The peace and quiet here belies the mills' violent past. The mills in their long history suffered several disastrous explosions. One in the 18th century badly damaged the roof of St Martha's church high on the hill above, while another in 1901 killed six workers. Continue along this peaceful path, ignoring a left fork, and pass an array of half buried grindstones and eventually go through the iron gates alongside West Lodge. This small cottage and gateway originally formed the factory entrance.

2. Turn right along the lane to cross two road bridges. When the road turns sharply right you should turn left for ten yards along a driveway and then right up an enclosed path. This is the start of our climb to St Martha's church, high on the greensand ridge 570 feet above the Tilling Bourne valley. At a small road continue ahead and pass Great Halfpenny Farm. Near the top of the incline by a house on your right called Southernway Cottage turn right up a sunken path, signposted 'North Downs Way'. Press on over a driveway and pass a single bar gate. Maintain direction on this wide, rising sandy track until the flint wall of St Martha's is reached. Turn right here and follow the wall to find seating for a well earned rest. Panoramic views across the Tilling

Bourne valley and also a glimpse of the Percy Arms below from whence the walk started are an additional reward for your exertions. After your rest continue along the wall to rejoin the North Downs Way. With your back to the chapel continue on a wide, downward sandy track between simple barred fences and pass a Second World War pillbox.

3. At a large junction of sandy tracks go half right, passing a post with a dragonfly motif, and 60 yards later turn right by a similar post. This narrow woodland path leads you downhill into the valley below. When the Tilling Bourne is reached the path continues left along a wide, raised pathway above the river through beautiful tranquil woodland. At posts by a house turn right along a tarmac drive, passing a mill pond on your left. Continue on this drive alongside a millstream and at the end of a development of housing and offices where once a mill and more recently a trout farm stood, turn right on a narrow fenced path by a small driveway. Cross a stile into a field and then maintain direction, crossing a further two fields with the remains of the Admiralty gunpowder mills, the last in use in this area, over to your right.

4. When a lane is reached turn left and retrace your steps to the Percy Arms and the end of the walk.

NEARBY ATTRACTIONS

Shalford Mill sits astride the Tilling Bourne at Shalford and basks in the richness of colour of its lovely half-tiled walls. Built in the 18th century the mill retains the original machinery including the waterwheel. Now owned by the National Trust it is open daily from 9.30 am to 5 pm and is situated 1 mile south of Guildford on the A281. Telephone: 01483 61617.

Chilworth Manor is a 17th-century manor house built by one of the owners of the gunpower mills in the valley below. In 1725 the Duchess of Marlborough acquired the manor and had the fine north front added in a classical red brick style. The house later fell into disrepair and was restored during the 1930s. Open between April and August from Wednesday to Sunday from 2 pm to 6 pm. Chilworth Manor is ⅓ mile east of the Percy Arms, off the A248.

THE RIVER WEY NAVIGATION
BY SHALFORD
❧

This beautiful and varied walk takes us along the banks of the River Wey to the south of Guildford. We pass 'The Wey Valley Meadows' - a Site of Special Scientific Interest. Southern marsh orchid, marsh marigold and ragged robin are just some of the plants that grow here and white admiral butterflies and elephant hawk moths are also to be found. Later the route passes picturesque Shalford Mill, a National Trust property.

A peaceful scene on the River Wey Navigation near Shalford

Shalford is named after a 'shallow ford' on the River Wey below St Catherine's Chapel on the route of what has become known as the Pilgrims' Way. In the early part of the 13th century, King John of Magna Carta fame gave a charter to the rector of Shalford to hold an annual fair. By 1287 it had outgrown its venue and was moved to Shalford Common. John Bunyan lived for a while in a cottage on the common and it is thought that he used it as a model for Vanity Fair in his *Pilgrim's Progress*, written in 1678. In the glory days of canals Shalford was a busy place for just south of Broadford Bridge is the junction of the Wey Navigation and the Wey and Arun Canal. It was here at Stonebridge Wharf that gunpowder from the Chilworth mills was loaded on barges for the journey to London. On a road named Pilgrims Way along our route we pass Cyder House Cottage, originally an old pesthouse – a term used to describe a plague hospital. Towards the end of the walk we pass the tile-hung Shalford Mill that sits astride the Tilling Bourne as it rushes on to meet the Wey just to the north of the village. The mill is now in the hands of the National Trust and is open daily to the public all year round.

The walk starts in Tillingbourne Road off The Street (A281) in Shalford. Just a few yards into the walk the route pass the Queen Victoria (telephone: 01483 561733), a Friary Meux public house where you will receive an excellent choice of home-made meals and traditional ales from the hand pump. A small walled garden is available for summer days. The Seahorse (telephone: 01483 514350), a much larger establishment offering superb food and ales, is passed towards the end of the walk so plenty of refreshment will be found on this easy and picturesque circuit.

- **HOW TO GET THERE:** Shalford is 1 mile south of Guildford on the A281. Tillingbourne Road is a turning off The Street, on your left just before the railway bridge if approaching from Guildford. If travelling by train the station is next to the Queen Victoria pub.

  Tillingbourne Buses and Thames Trains serve the village.
- **PARKING:** There is plenty of parking in Tillingbourne Road. Alternative parking will be found a few yards past the railway bridge to the right by a scout hut.
- **LENGTH OF THE WALK:** 3 miles. Map: OS Landranger 186 Aldershot, Guildford and surrounding area (GR 001471).

THE WALK

1. From Tillingbourne Road walk out to the busy A281 and go left to cross the railway bridge. After 80 yards go right along a lane alongside a parking area and scout hut. At a fork in the lane keep ahead and soon turn right and cross a second railway bridge. Ignore a path immediately on your left and continue ahead until the top of a small incline is reached where you go through a kissing gate on your left. Continue

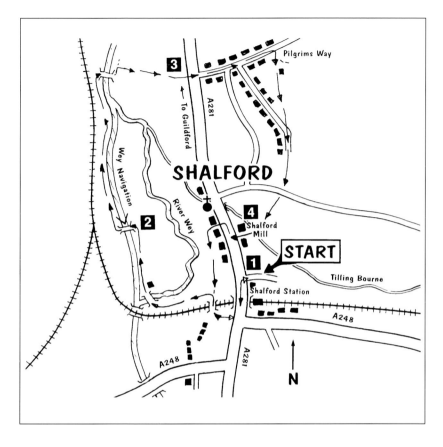

downhill to marshy ground below and carry on along a raised boarded pathway to reach the bank of the River Wey. Bear leftwards along the river and cross a bridge to your right by a weir. Now continue through a small gate alongside the Wey Navigation with The Wey Valley Meadows on your right.

2. When a lock is reached cross a bridge and press on along the left bank of the Navigation. Glimpses of St Catherine's Chapel may be seen high on a hill ahead. A vertical roller is passed along the way that enabled horse-drawn barges to negotiate the sharp bend. Soon after passing sand cliffs with St Catherine's Chapel atop go right over a rather unsightly bridge. Continue in the same direction on the right bank for 50 yards and then go rightwards on a path that leads you directly away from the river. Continue over a large grassy area to reach the A281 by a double gate and seat.

73

3. Cross the road with caution and press on ahead along a residential road named Pilgrims Way. Near the top end of this road to your left is Cyder House Cottage. At a bend in the road turn rightwards along a driveway signposted 'North Downs Way'. Soon after passing a parking area and by Chantry Cottage turn right on a footpath. Ignore the entrance to Chantry Wood and continue along this charming path that in spring is lined with red campion, herb Robert and speedwell. Finally when a small road is reached continue leftwards along it. At the end of this road go left to meet a dirt track to soon meet a road. Cross a stile at the far side of the road and maintain direction over a field to a further stile. Cross this stile and go forward on an enclosed path to pass Shalford Mill and reach the A281 by the Seahorse public house.

4. Turn right along the road and then left to a public bridleway when opposite the end of the pub car park. After going between posts bear leftwards on a path signposted to Godalming. Continue along this wide path until the railway bridge is reached where you should now retrace your steps to Tillingbourne Road and the end of the walk.

NEARBY ATTRACTIONS

Clandon Park is the seat of one of Surrey's great families, the Onslows. The house designed by Giacomo Leoni was built around 1730 and the grounds laid out by Capability Brown. A feature of the house is the Marble Hall where plasterwork imitates marble. The National Trust now owns the property which is open from the beginning of April to the end of October, Tuesday to Thursday, Sunday and bank holiday Monday, Good Friday and Easter Saturday. Clandon Park is 2 miles east of Guildford on the A25. Telephone: 01483 222482.

Loseley House, built from the remains of Waverley Abbey in 1562 for Sir William More, is still owned by Sir William's descendants. Panelling from Henry VIII's Nonsuch Palace is incorporated in the Great Hall. Open from May to October, Wednesday to Saturday and bank holidays from 2 pm to 5 pm. Loseley House is situated 3 miles west of Guildford off the B3000. Telephone: 01483 304440.

Guildford Boat House in Millbrook, just a few minutes walk from Guildford High Street, offers boats and canoes for hire in the summer months, as well as short river trips. There is also a floating restaurant. Telephone: 01483 504494.

THE RIVER WEY AND GODALMING NAVIGATION BY CATTESHALL

This picturesque and peaceful walk is along a part of the River Wey Navigation that was built in 1760 and later linked Godalming to the Wey and Arun Canal, giving the town - a centre for the wool and tanning industries - direct access to London and the south coast. This once bustling industrial waterway has been revived by the National Trust who aim to preserve the now peaceful and unspoilt nature of the canal. Many colourful waterside plants are seen along the bank and in the water meadows. In summer the canal bank offers many delightful spots for those who wish to picnic and while away an afternoon watching the occasional narrow boat or rowing boat pass.

Catteshall Lock

The walk passes Farncombe Boat House where you may hire a canoe, rowing boat or even a narrow boat for a day's messing about on the water. In summer and at weekends in the winter refreshments are served in the pretty tea rooms adjoining the working boatyard where narrow boats are fitted out and repaired (telephone: 01483 421306). A captivating sight along the canal hereabouts is the horse-drawn *Iona*. Built originally in 1935 for the Grand Union Carrying Company this 70 foot narrow boat has been converted for passenger use and now offers two-hour canal trips from Easter to the end of September that depart from Godalming Wharf.

The walk starts at the Leathern Bottle, a small, friendly pub built around 1896. Draught beers include Webster's, Hogs Back, Boddingtons, Courage Best, Guinness, Murphy's, Heineken, Holsten, Stella and Foster's – a pretty comprehensive range that should cover all tastes – plus wine by the glass and bottle. A choice of wholesome food is available from either the bar, children's or vegetarian menu. There is a small beer garden where you can relax in the summer sun. Telephone: 01483 425642.

- **HOW TO GET THERE:** The Leathern Bottle stands in Meadrow (A3100) just ½ mile north-east of the centre of Godalming. If travelling from Guildford take the A3100 and after 3½ miles, next to a pay and display car park on your right, you will see the Leathern Bottle pub.
  Tillingbourne Buses serve the area.
- **PARKING:** Those using the facilities of the Leathern Bottle may leave their car in the small pub car park. There is also plenty of additional parking in the pay and display car park next door (free on Sundays) or limited parking in Catteshall Road opposite.
- **LENGTH OF THE WALK:** 2¼ miles. Map: OS Landranger 186 Aldershot, Guildford and surrounding area (GR 980448).

THE WALK

1. From the Leathern Bottle cross the busy A3100 to Catteshall Road opposite which you continue along. At a road bridge by Farncombe Boat House go through an iron gate on your left and follow the towpath. Many pretty narrow boats are moored along the far bank here, some awaiting repair. At a small bridge, continue ahead along the towpath, passing the rear of fine houses, and soon the canal passes through beautiful water meadows where there is an abundance of purple loosestrife, Himalayan balsam and the less significant, but no less beautiful, orange balsam.

2. At a second bridge turn right along the road and in a short distance, after crossing two bridges in quick succession, turn right into Unstead

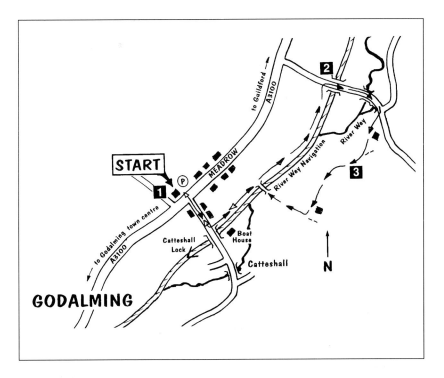

Lane. After 30 yards cross a stile on your right and walk diagonally left to a stile in the field edge some 50 yards or so past a large black barn. Carry on along a fenced path to soon cross another stile and turn right along a cart track.

3. When the cart track ends by a gate go ahead along a fenced path between fields with fine views across the water meadows to the canal beyond. Soon after passing a house, turn right at a junction of tracks and press on to reach the canal bank by a bridge. Cross the bridge and turn left along the towpath to retrace your steps back to Farncombe Boat House where, after turning right along Catteshall Road, the Leathern Bottle and the end of the walk are reached.

NEARBY ATTRACTION

The Godalming Packetboat Company offers two-hour trips along the canal aboard the *Iona*, a traditional narrow boat pulled by one of their three heavy horses. All trips depart and return from Godalming Wharf near the Sainsburys store. Telephone: 01483 425397.

TILFORD, THE RIVER WEY AND FRENSHAM LITTLE POND
❦

This peaceful and mainly woodland walk starts alongside the 13th-century bridge built at Tilford by the monks of nearby Waverley Abbey. The River Wey North and South Branches meet in the water meadow just beyond the bridge to combine their force as the river makes its way towards Elstead. You will stroll by both branches on this circular route and there is also a chance to sit awhile and enjoy the birdlife of Frensham Little Pond, a delightful spot at any time of year.

The 13th-century bridge over the River Wey, Tilford

Tilford is blessed with one of the best greens in Surrey. It is triangular in shape and contains a lovely cricket pitch where the game has been played for well over 100 years. There is an oak tree by the green – reputedly 'the oak at Kynghoc', mentioned in the charter of Waverley Abbey in 1128. Whilst this may be in some doubt, what is not is its great age. In 1822 William Cobbett described it as 'the finest tree I ever saw in my life'. How times have changed, with most of its boughs gone and partially clad in metal sheeting to keep the weather out, it is truly a sad sight. On another side of the green is the River Wey where in summer months children paddle in the shallow waters of its ford alongside the aged bridge. Our walk includes a visit to Frensham Little Pond where reed warblers, great crested grebes and herons make their home as well as tufted ducks, pochards and golden-eyes. The surrounding 400 hectares of Frensham Common are also home to Dartford warblers, woodlarks, silver studded blue butterflies and sand lizards.

The walk starts by the Barley Mow public house on Tilford green. This welcoming pub was originally built in the 18th century as a pair of cottages and overlooks the cricket pitch – reputedly the second oldest in England. William Beldham, 'Silver Billy', the greatest cricketer of his time, retired from the game in 1822 and became the landlord of the Barley Mow. It is said that his ghost still appears in the pub from time to time. Later he moved into Oak Cottage by the famous old oak tree. If you are lucky enough to visit this traditional village pub at the right time you will be entertained by morris dancers. There is a selection of guest ales from the local Hogs Back Brewery and a wide choice of home cooking available, with children and vegetarians fully catered for. An à la carte menu is available during the evenings and it is advisable to book if wishing to eat here on Saturday or Sunday evenings. A pleasant garden and patio overlook the river at the rear of this popular pub. Telephone: 01252 792205.

- **HOW TO GET THERE:** From the A3 south of Guildford follow the B3001 to Elstead. Continue through Elstead and cross a bridge and pass Elstead Mill. After the road dips by the Donkey public house take the second turning on your left – Green Lane, signposted to Tilford. At a T-junction turn left again and continue until crossing the narrow bridge by Tilford green where the Barley Mow is ahead of you.

  From Farnham take the B3001 in the direction of Elstead and the A3. After passing the ruins of Waverley Abbey take the first turning on your right, signposted to Tilford. Continue on this road until crossing the narrow bridge by Tilford green.

  Tillingbourne Buses serve the village.
- **PARKING:** In the road by the Barley Mow or in the parking area alongside the river.

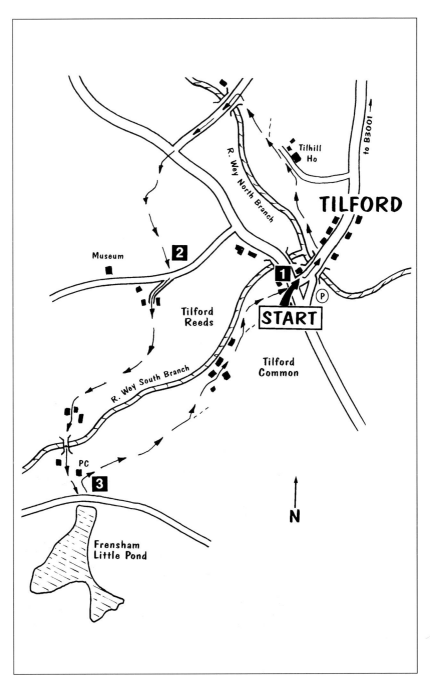

- **LENGTH OF THE WALK:** 4 miles. Map: OS Landranger 186 Aldershot, Guildford and surrounding area (GR 874434).

THE WALK

1. With your back to the Barley Mow go left to the ancient narrow bridge and after crossing it turn left on a fenced path alongside the Post Office and General Stores. Within yards you may just see across the water meadow where both branches of the river converge. This gently sloping uphill path follows the line of the River Wey North Branch. When a small lane is reached maintain direction and soon pass lovely Tilhill House. Continue into woodland at the end of the lane and at a fork keep ahead and left. Eventually the path drops down to the river by a road bridge. Turn left along this quiet lane and continue to a T-junction where after crossing a road you press on ahead through trees on a signposted path. This path passes through lovely woodland as it skirts fields over to your left.

2. At a road, continue on a cart track ahead and right. After passing two houses and stabling the track narrows as it again goes through trees. Soon the path broadens as it continues through well managed woodland to eventually reach a farm where, after going through a gate

The Barley Mow alongside the superb green at Tilford

and between farm buildings, we pass the farmhouse to soon reach the River Wey South Branch. Cross the footbridge and continue along a farm track, passing an attractive cottage. At a fork keep left and soon at a junction of paths alongside public conveniences press on ahead to reach the bank of Frensham Little Pond. The pond is well worth a visit. As it is just over the halfway mark of the walk it also makes a convenient picnic spot.

3. Leaving the delights of Frensham Little Pond behind you, retrace your steps to the public conveniences where you now turn right on a broad track, passing a post inscribed with the number 522. In ⅓ mile and soon after passing a bridleway on the right, turn left over a stile and continue along a fenced path. When farm buildings are reached keep ahead and left on a broad cart track and pass two houses. Across to your left you may glimpse the River Wey South Branch. Pass a third house and soon fork left on a narrow path between holly bushes. This path finally joins the river in a beautiful bluebell wood. At a gate go forward on a fenced path with the planting area of Tilford Green Nursery on your right. At a driveway continue out to a road which you cross to Tilford green. To your left is the famous old oak tree and just a few yards on the Barley Mow and the end of the walk.

NEARBY ATTRACTIONS

Old Kiln Museum is a private collection of farm implements and machinery. Included is a complete Sussex wheelwright's shop, smithy and hop bagging machine. There is also a good collection of horse-drawn ploughs. The museum is in Reeds Road, Tilford, ¾ mile west of the village, and is open in the summer months. Telephone for times: 01252 792300.

Farnham Castle Keep is a 12th-century motte and bailey castle open to the public. The large shell keep encloses a mound which contains the massive foundations of a Norman tower. The castle is located in Castle Hill, ½ mile north of the town centre, and is open from 1st April to 1st November, 10 am to dusk. Telephone: 01252 713393.

WALK 18

THE WEY AND ARUN CANAL AND WEY SOUTH PATH
ᴥᏸᏸᴥ

This excellent walk traces a part of the the Wey and Arun Canal that once linked the River Thames to the south coast at Littlehampton. It is unfortunate that only one small section of canal still contains water. Ironically, for some of the way the dry canal bed is viewed from the Wey South Path that runs along the track of a disused railway which itself is now unused and unwanted. The route passes through magnificent countryside near Shamley Green.

The Red Lion, Shamley Green

The walk starts at picturesque Shamley Green, an archetype Surrey village once known as Shamble Lea. Many fine and interesting houses are charmingly laid out around the outstanding green which is bisected by the main road that separates the cricket pitch from the duck pond. The Romans occupied the area during the 1st century AD and just a mile to the east at Farley Heath are the remains of a large Romano-

British temple. Several finds of Roman coins have been discovered around the village in recent times. During the 17th century Oliver Cromwell bestowed on Shamble Lea a charter to hold an annual fair.

The Wey and Arun Canal opened for business in 1816 and linked the Wey Navigation at Stonebridge near Godalming to the river Arun near Billingshurst, thereby forming the 'inland link' to the south coast. Due to rapid improvements in the road system at that time the full potential of the canal was never realised and it survived for little more than fifty years. The fate of all canals in the south of England generally was sealed by the ever increasing competition from railways.

The Red Lion in the centre of Shamley Green is a picturesque grade 2 listed building that was formally a coach house and inn. Situated opposite the village cricket green, it has a pleasant garden and patio where you can relax in the summer sun. There is all-day opening throughout the week, with coffee available from 7 am (8 am on Sundays) even before the bar opens. Beers and lagers on tap include Young's, Flowers, Abbot Ale, Murphy's, Carlsberg, 4X and Lowenbrau. Wine is also available by the glass or bottle. A wide selection of food is available from a bar snack menu, children's menu and à la carte menu with a smaller selection of vegetarian dishes on offer. Booking is advisable for à la carte meals. Telephone: 01483 892202.

- **HOW TO GET THERE:** Shamley Green is 4 miles south of Guildford and straddles the B2128. When travelling south, the Red Lion public house is situated to your left at the beginning of the village green.
  Arriva Buses serve the village.
- **PARKING:** Walkers using the Red Lion may leave their cars in the pub car park. Alternative parking will be found around the green.
- **LENGTH OF THE WALK:** 5 miles. Map: OS Landranger 186, Aldershot, Guildford and surrounding area (GR 032439).

THE WALK

1. With your back to the Red Lion, cross the main road and continue to the left of the cricket pitch to reach Hullbrook Lane. Press on along this quiet lane and ignore a footpath on your right. After passing the entrance way to Longacre Preparatory School a small road junction is reached where you turn left on a tarmac bridleway, passing between a lovely house named Hullhatch and a small pond. Keep ahead on this enchanting bridleway where in spring the profuse banks of red campion are unsurpassed.

84

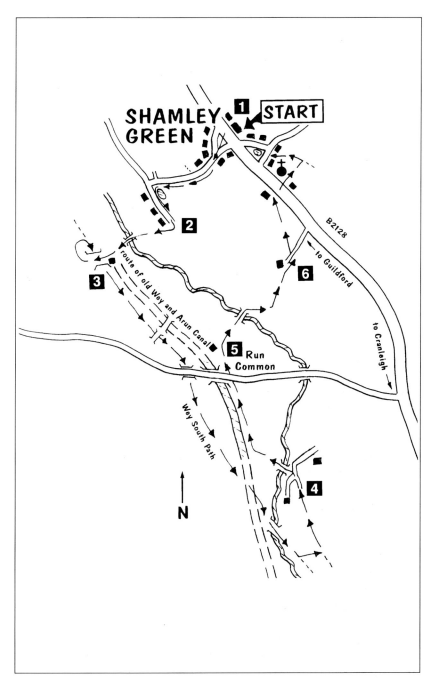

2. Soon after passing the entrance to Oriel Cottage turn right on a grass bridleway that goes through trees to a gate. Continue beyond the gate along a fenced path that leads you over a small bridge that crosses a tributary of the River Wey. Now bear half right along a field edge to reach a gate which you pass through to continue along a farm track. After passing Fansesbridge Cottage turn right through a gate and descend down steps to reach the bed of a disused railway line that now forms the Downs Link long distance footpath and also a part of the Wey South Path. Turn right here. For much of the way this old railway line follows the dried-up remains of the Wey and Arun Canal which can be seen over to your left.

3. Continue along this pleasant pathway for 1¼ miles, passing under two brick bridges along the way. Towards the end of this section you will notice a brick parapet where the track passes over the canal which now continues to your right. Soon after the pathway passes over a small river – the tributary we crossed earlier – turn left over a stile and continue ahead to the crest of an incline to an amusing horse jump. When this is reached go left along a broad bridleway that offers fine views to Hascombe Hill on your left and Pitch Hill on your right.

4. When a small lane is reached continue rightwards along it and as it turns to the right go left through a gate and then diagonally right to cross a small bridge. Continue ahead on an indistinct path to the top of the field where you now turn right along the field edge. Shortly, cross a stile and maintain direction along what was once the towpath of the canal. Cross a road and continue beside the canal.

5. When the canal abruptly ends by a house turn right on a broad grassy farm track. Continue through a gate and soon pass an old cattle shed to reach a further gate. Go through this to cross a small bridge and then proceed diagonally right across a field to a further gate which you pass through. Press on ahead along a lovely path that passes through a ribbon of trees.

6. At an entrance way to a house continue ahead along a drive for 80 yards and then turn left over a stile into a field. Keep to the right-hand field edge and as the field opens out maintain direction ahead to a stile at the crest of the hill. Cross this and maintain direction over a second field to reach a stile in the far corner alongside a road. Continue ahead along a raised bank that runs parallel to the road. When this path ends, cross the road and continue along an enclosed path between a large house and a church. Maintain direction through fields via kissing gates and at a T-junction turn left along a narrow holly-lined path that passes alongside gardens to finally reach the village green, the Red Lion pub and the end of the walk.

NEARBY ATTRACTION

Winkworth Arboretum: this wonderful setting always has something worth seeing no matter what the time of year, and for late spring colour it would be hard to find a better location for azaleas. The tree and shrub covered hills are reflected in the mirror-like surface of the delightful lake. Many water birds are to been seen here and you may get a glimpse of the occasional kingfisher. Open all year round during daylight hours, Winkworth Arboretum can be found 3 miles south of Godalming on the B2130. Telephone: 01483 208477.

THURSLEY NATURE RESERVE AND PONDS

The very soil that makes Thursley Nature Reserve a site of international ecological importance has saved it from the development that has overtaken other parts of Surrey. This is a waterside walk with a difference as soon after the route leaves the starting point alongside the Moat pond we explore the famous Thursley bog from boardwalks that make this area accessible . The drier and equally important areas of the nature reserve are viewed from lovely broad sandy tracks. Three further ponds are passed along the route of this interesting and enthralling walk.

A boarded walkway through the famous bog

Thursley Nature Reserve is one of the largest surviving remnants of heathland in Surrey. The 800 acres covered by this reserve offer wildly contrasting habitats that include wetland bog, heath and woodland. The area is well known for its diverse wildlife and 26 species of dragonfly have been identified and many rare birds and reptiles make their home in this unique habitat. Now that cattle no longer graze here English Nature periodically remove young tree saplings and cut back the heather to improve its long-term vigour in order to maintain the delicate balance of the heathland.

After starting alongside the Moat pond – a place teeming with water birds and wildlife – the route follows boardwalks through a part of the bog where during summer, myriads of tiny glistening sundew will be seen awaiting unsuspecting insects among the sphagnum moss. Also growing along here is the delicate bog asphodel, marsh orchid and St John's wort. During early autumn the heath glows with many shades of pink and mauve as the heather comes into flower. Even in the depths of winter there is plenty to see. I well remember one damp misty morning walking through here and marvelling at the trees and gorse bushes which were adorned with hundreds of magnificent spiders webs weighed down with pearls of dew and each reflecting the early morning sun.

After crossing the bog the route follows a level track through lovely pine woodland before passing the still waters of Warren Mere, the halfway point of the walk and an ideal spot for a picnic. Soon after this another pond is visited where you will see quite clearly how the valley was dammed to form a hammer pond. This hammer pond was one of the driving forces for the iron industry that flourished here from about the mid 1500s. Around the area are shallow depressions in the sandy soil that mark where early settlers dug out iron-ore for the furnaces. Later, in 1794 the pond drove a silk mill until it closed in 1870. The route then returns to the Moat pond via a scenic path across Thursley Common where the observant walker may catch a glimpse of a rare bird or two.

- **HOW TO GET THERE:** From the A3 six miles south of Guildford take the B3001 to Elstead and at the small triangular village green turn left into Thursley Road. After 1½ miles the Moat car park will be seen on your left.
  Stagecoach Hants & Surrey and Tillingbourne Buses serve the area.
- **PARKING:** At the Moat pond.
- **LENGTH OF THE WALK:** 4¼ miles. Map: OS Landranger 186 Aldershot, Guildford and surrounding area (GR 899416).

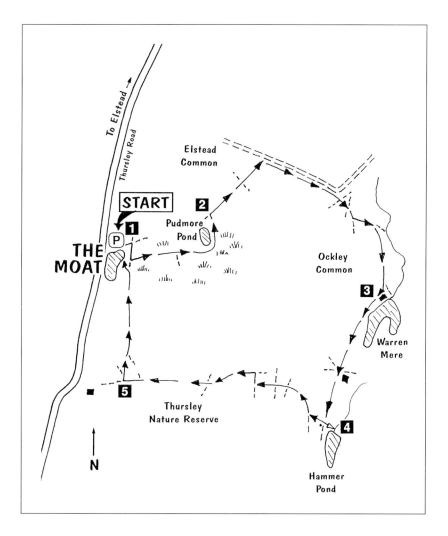

THE WALK

1. With your back to the car park and with the banks of the Moat on your right pass between pine trees on a broad sandy track. Soon turn right at a junction of tracks under power cables. After about 150 yards turn left on a narrower path alongside a Thursley Nature Reserve sign. This path now leads you through a part of the nationally famous bog via a series of boardwalks. Later, unless you wish to visit a dragonfly identification information point, ignore a boardwalk on your right and keep ahead along the causeway. Finally after passing around Pudmore

Pond and following a line of pine trees with rather exposed roots a T-junction is met.

2. Turn right at this T-junction and press on along a broad sandy track towards a stand of pines in the distance. Ignore paths on either side and maintain direction until a cart track is met. Turn right along this pleasant cart track and ignore paths to left and right. When the track bends sharply leftwards by power cables at a junction of tracks keep ahead on an unmade wide path. In a short distance at a second junction of tracks keep ahead maintaining direction. Soon, by an English Nature Reserve sign turn left on a sandy path and in 80 yards bear right at a fork. The path now leads you through stands of tall Scots pine and towards the edge of a field. Continue rightwards when this field is met and ignore a bridleway on your left by a gate.

3. At a fork in the path alongside a large barn bear right and before long the shimmering waters of Warren Mere will be seen through the trees to your left. This lake marks the halfway point of the walk and is a lovely spot for a picnic. Our way continues along the bridleway which before long follows a small bank and fence on your left. At a junction of paths press on along the line of the fence and soon pass a house set amongst the trees. Finally when this small fence ends by a junction of paths and a post, turn leftwards to visit the still waters of the Hammer pond. You will see quite clearly where the valley was dammed to create the driving force for Thursley's iron-works.

4. Retrace your steps back to the junction of tracks and the post. With your back to the Hammer pond cross the bridleway you have been following and continue ahead on a narrow path up an incline. Soon a stony crossing path is met where you should now turn right along it. This lovely path offers views over Thursley Common and gives you the opportunity to spot the rare birds that nest and hunt here. At a broad sandy crossing track keep ahead on your original path. Press on over a second crossing track and keep roughly parallel to power cables. Pass through a small piece of oak woodland on a well defined path to soon meet a broad sandy track at a T-junction. Turn right here for 50 yards and at a second T-junction turn left. You will notice that you are still following the line of power cables. Keep ahead and ignore any side paths until you spot a gate across the bridleway some 150 yards ahead of you.

5. With the gate 150 yards ahead of you turn right on a sandy bridleway and ignore a left fork. Soon, as this track is met by another coming in from your right, maintain direction. Keep to this wide track as it skirts Thursley Common and look out for the Thursley Nature Reserve sign you passed earlier. Turn left here on a narrower path through trees and soon at a fork bear right and within yards you will discover the bank of the Moat with the car park and the end of the walk ahead of you.

NEARBY ATTRACTION

Ramster Gardens was laid out in 1904 and contains 20 acres of woodland, and flowering shrub garden. The privately owned and well maintained gardens include a pretty lake with bog garden. Dogs are allowed in the grounds if on a lead and there are plants for sale. The gardens are open from mid-April to mid-July from 11 am to 5.30 pm. Ramster Gardens are to be found 1½ miles south of Chiddingfold off the A283. Telephone 01428 654167.

THE HEADWATERS OF THE RIVER ARUN BY DUNSFOLD

This outstanding field and woodland walk around Dunsfold passes through picturesque undulating scenery that is typical of this corner of Surrey. Several small brooks join with the infant River Arun - the great Sussex river - and together they cut a deep gully through the beautiful indigenous woodland that flourishes in this area. Fine houses, some dating back to the 17th century, are passed along the way and a small diversion takes you to a Holy Well once believed to provide cures for eye disorders.

The infant River Arun cutting its way through the wooded valley

Because of the abundance of timber, white sand and water power, this part of Surrey became an important centre for glassmaking between the 13th and 17th centuries. The woodland in this area was heavily used for burning charcoal, so essential for its manufacture. Over the centuries the woodland around Dunsfold has at various times supported not only the glass furnaces but also local ironworks and later a government gunpowder works. Towards the end of the walk, the route passes Dunsfold church where almost nothing has changed in the last 700 years. Contained within is the original font and the present day congregation sit on the original 13th-century pews said to be the oldest in Britain.

The walk starts at the Sun Inn on Dunsfold Common. This lovely village pub, once a coaching inn, sits handsomely back from the road that dissects the common and separates the pub from the cricket pitch. Parts of the charming building date back to the 15th and 17th centuries. An old time atmosphere exudes from the open fires and good home cooking. Beers on tap include Friary Meux Best Bitter, King & Barnes Sussex Ale and Marston's Pedigree Bitter while wine is served by the glass or bottle. A good selection of food is served from the bar and à la carte menus with a choice of vegetarian dishes are available. Booking is advisable at weekends during the summer. There is a garden and patio area for you to relax in during pleasant weather. Telephone: 01483 200242.

- **HOW TO GET THERE:** Dunsfold is approximately 6 miles south of Guildford off the A281. Turn off westwards at Nanhurst crossroads onto the B2130 and in 1 mile turn left on a road signposted to Dunsfold. A further mile on and Dunsfold Green is met where the Sun Inn will be found to your right.

  Tillingbourne Buses serve the village.
- **PARKING:** There is ample parking around the green outside the Sun Inn.
- **LENGTH OF THE WALK:** 5½ miles. Map: OS Landranger 186 Aldershot, Guildford and surrounding area (GR 005363).

THE WALK

1. When facing the Sun Inn go leftwards to meet Oak Tree Lane and continue along it, passing the famous old oak tree – a Dunsfold landmark for many centuries. Press on past lovely old Oak Tree and Pond Cottages to soon reach and pass a group of bungalows. At the end of the lane continue ahead on a broad path through oak woodland where you soon meet and cross the infant River Arun. Continue ahead and soon a farm track is reached alongside The Mill House. Maintain direction ahead along the track for about ⅓ mile and immediately after passing a remote bungalow turn right on a footpath between rhododendron trees. Soon turn right on a smaller signposted path that leads you gently down to the valley floor and the River Arun.

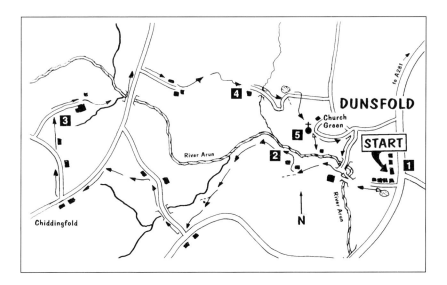

2. This lovely path follows the river as it snakes through mixed woodland alive with the sound of birdsong, a far cry from those distant days of continual felling and charcoal burning that once kept the local furnaces working. Press on along this path with the river to your right. After a short incline a post is reached by a fork in the path. Take the left fork and continue uphill to reach a small junction of roads. Turn right and follow the small lane as it goes downhill to soon cross the water. Continue along the lane as it then makes the short climb out of this small wooded valley. Eighty yards after passing the entrance to White Beech Farm take a bridleway to your left that follows a ribbon of trees between fields to reach another small lane. Turn left along the lane and soon at a road junction by a house turn right along another small lane, signposted to Godalming. In a short while at a left bend and alongside a large barn, continue ahead and right on a bridleway that leads you past Yew Tree Cottage. Go through a field gate and continue forward on the right-hand field edge. Exit this field via a stile alongside a drive.

3. Turn right along this drive and pass the outbuildings of Stonehurst, a fine old country farmhouse. Press on along the drive, passing an old grain store – the inscription under the door gives some clue as to its age. Soon pass a lovely pond and cross a stile where you continue ahead through a long narrow field along the valley bottom. Cross a stile at the end of this field followed by two others in quick succession.

Keep ahead on a fenced path to soon reach a road. Turn left here and in 250 yards turn right on a bridleway along a track that leads to Pockford Farm. At farm buildings go left with the track and soon when it bends to the right press on ahead through a gate and stay on the left-hand field edge. At the end of this field go through a gate into a second field and turn right to follow the right-hand field edge. At a further gate go diagonally right to a third field and remain on the left. Soon you should take a narrow path to reach a house.

4. Pass the front of the house and continue along the unmade driveway and soon after crossing a stream go left over a stile into a field and continue diagonally right uphill to a further stile which you cross. Press on leftwards along the drive, soon passing a duckpond. Ignore a stile by the pond and continue along the drive to reach a junction of field gates where you now go right over a stile. Stay on the right-hand field edge to eventually reach a stile in the far corner. Cross this next field diagonally rightwards to a stile half hidden in the corner. Go over the stile to enter Dunsfold churchyard and proceed leftwards alongside the church to reach a fine yew arch and lychgate.

5. Exit the churchyard via the lychgate and press on along the road. (If you wish to visit the Holy Well turn immediately right on a footpath by the lychgate. In approximately 200 yards the River Arun and the shrine will be reached. Retrace your steps to the lychgate and continue rightwards along the road.) At a T-junction turn right along the road and in 50 yards turn right again along a drive leading to The Mill House. When the drive crosses the river turn left and retrace your steps back to the Sun Inn and the end of the walk.

NEARBY ATTRACTION
The Countryways Experience was once a working farm. It is now a farm museum and a place where all the family can enjoy an afternoon or a day out. Children can feed most of the small animals including lambs, goats and piglets. There are pony and tractor rides plus an indoor and outdoor play area. For those of us a little older there are woodland walks, a Victorian walled garden, farm shop and tea room. The museum is open from the beginning of February until the end of October, from 10.30 am to 5 pm every weekend and every day during the school holidays.Take the small road opposite the the Sun Inn and in 1½ miles follow the Countryways sign. Telephone: 01403 753589.